DATE DUE

Modern Critical Interpretations

Modern Critical Interpretations

Albert Camus's
The Stranger

Edited and with an introduction by

Harold Bloom
Sterling Professor of the Humanities
Yale University

CHELSEA HOUSE PUBLISHERS
Philadelphia

Printed and bound in the United States of America

10 9 8 7 6 5 4 3 2 1

∞ The paper used in this publication meets the minimum requirements of the American National Standard for Permanence of Paper for Printed Library Materials, Z39.48-1984

Library of Congress Cataloging-in-Publication Data

Albert Camus's The Stranger / Harold Bloom, editor.
     p. cm. — (Modern critical interpretations)
   Includes bibliographical references and index.
   ISBN 0-7910-5928-6 (alk. paper)
   1. Camus, Albert, 1913-1960. Etranger. I. Bloom, Harold. II. Series
PQ2605.A3734 E8335   2000
843'.914—dc21   00-060306
                                       CIP

Chelsea House Publishers
1974 Sproul Road, Suite 400
Broomall, PA 19008-0914

The Chelsea House World Wide Web address is
http://www.chelseahouse.com

Contributing Editor: Mirjana Kalezic

Produced by: Robert Gerson Publisher's Services, Avondale, PA

Contents

Editor's Note

My Introduction centers upon Meursault as a man who does not deserve execution.

Sartre stresses *The Stranger*'s connection to *The Myth of Sisyphus*, while Camus himself defends Meursault as a figure who refuses to lie.

The novelist Robbe-Grillet, in a view much like my own, absorbs Meursault into nature, after which Germaine Brée exalts Meursault as a hero.

Roger Shattuck analogizes *Billy Budd* and *The Stranger*, while Robert Champigny broods upon ethical considerations.

The fierce moralist René Girard denounces Meursault as a mindless killer, after which William M. Manly expands upon Sartre's views.

A. D. Nuttall seeks to mitigate Meursault's guilt, while David Sprintzen confines himself to structural analysis.

Peter Schofer discourses upon irony, after which the philosophical background of Meursault's behavior is indicated by Frantz Favre.

In this volume's final essay, Stephen Eric Bonner attributes rather more affect to Meursault than most readers tend to find.

Introduction

Albert Camus wrote and published *L'Etranger* before he was thirty. Only forty-six when he was killed in a car crash, Camus might seem an unfulfilled novelist, except that he was always essentially an essayist, even in his narrative fictions. *The Stranger* (which loses little in the eloquent translation of Mathew Ward) inflicts a considerable wound at first reading. I have just reread it after twelve years, and am a touch saddened by its imaginative inadequacy, yet remain moved by its protagonist's pragmatic innocence. Meursault may be an odd version of Voltaire's Candide, but Jean Paul Sartre's insight remains correct, and *The Stranger*, no comedy, clearly has its affinity with Voltaire's "philosophical" fables, *Candide* and *Zadig*. An emblematic rather than enigmatic figure, Meursault compares poorly with Dostoevsky's fierce nihilists or with Kafka's guilty obsessives. An admirer of Melville and of Faulkner, Camus could not begin to match the terrifying Shakespearean inwardness of Captain Ahab or of Darl Bundren (*As I Lay Dying*). Lucid, severe, and engaging, *The Stranger* nevertheless is a tendentious work, one that knows too well what it is about, and what its effect upon the reader will be.

"We have to labor and to struggle to reconquer solitude." That is Camus in his *Notebooks* in September 1937, when he was going on twenty-four. We need not consider Camus the most authentic spokesman of aesthetic solitude in the century just past—that distinction belongs to Franz Kafka, rightly considered by W. H. Auden to have been the Dante of his age. Kafka, desperate for happiness, found next to none. Camus, who thought of himself as happy, can seem a minor moralist when compared to Kafka, or to Freud. And yet Camus became the most representative intellectual of the 1950s, both in France and throughout the West. He stood for individualism: moral, aesthetic, social, political, and for the ultimate value of each person's consciousness, however absurd (or absurdist) such consciousness might be.

And yet time has dimmed Camus, particularly as a literary artist. Forty years after his death, we read him as an incarnation of the Fifties, not as a seer of Eternity, like Kafka or like Samuel Beckett. On the scale of a James Joyce or a Marcel Proust, Camus' fictions fade out of existence. Is Camus now more than a nostalgia, and is *The Stranger* still a poignant and persuasive narrative? A period piece can have its own value, but time at last will efface it.

I first read *The Stranger* in 1948, when I was eighteen, and was strongly moved. Returning to it in 1988, I was rather disappointed; time seemed to have worn it smooth. Reading it a third time, in 2000, I find I hover between my two earlier critical impressions. The book's stance refreshes me, as it did not twelve years ago, even though I cannot recapture the curious vividness *The Stranger* seemed to possess more than half-a-century back. *Then* it seemed tragic, though on a minor scale, an aesthetic dignity I could not locate in 1988. Tragedy, in 2000, clearly is too large a notion to apply to Meursault. Camus regards him as essentially innocent, but if Meursault is nature's victim, or society's rather than of some element in his self, then who would think him tragic? And yet Camus presents Meursault, extreme though he be, as a valid self, one that ought to survive. This is a subtle test for the reader, since Meursault is just barely sympathetic. At first, indeed, Meursault's is an inadequate consciousness as, dazed by the North African sun, Meursault murders a man, gratuitously, and evidently without willing himself to do so. Though he never feels, or expresses, remorse for the murder, Meursault changes as he undergoes legal judgment and approaches execution. Everything had been all the same to Meursault; he had seemed incapable of wanting anything very much, or wanting it more than another thing. As he awaits death, Meursault affirms a version of self: the knowing pariah who wants only the enmity of the state and the people.

Camus makes Meursault into someone we are in no position to judge, but that is an aesthetic risk, because can we still care when we are not competent to at least reach for judgment? Christianity is massively irrelevant to *The Stranger*, and to all of Camus' work. Secular humanism, now out of fashion, is affirmed throughout Camus, and in 2000 I am touched by the desperate minimalism of Meursault. To see that even Meursault ought to be allowed to go on, is to see again the obscenity of capital punishment. The United States, these days, executes on a fairly grand scale. Texas alone, guided by Governor George W. Bush, incessantly takes away human life. In 2000, *The Stranger* ironically becomes a strong parable against the death penalty. Meursault is not as yet an impressive person as his book closes, but he *has* begun to change, to feel, to choose, to will. To destroy him is more than a societal blunder, in Camus' view. Meursault's life has been an absurdity, but to take away his life is even more absurd.

An Explication of The Stranger

Camus's *The Stranger* was barely off the press when it began to arouse the widest interest. People told each other that it was "the best book since the end of the war." Amidst the literary productions of its time, this novel was, itself, a stranger. It came to us from the other side of the Equator, from across the sea. In that bitter spring of the coal shortage, it spoke to us of the sun, not as of an exotic marvel, but with the weary familiarity of those who have had too much of it. It was not concerned with re-burying the old regime with its own hands, nor with filling us with a sense of our own unworthiness.

We remembered, while reading this novel, that there had once been works which had not tried to prove anything, but had been content to stand on their own merits. But hand in hand with its gratuitousness went a certain ambiguity. How were we to interpret this character who, the day after his mother's death, "went swimming, started a liaison with a girl and went to see a comic film," who killed an Arab "because of the sun," who claimed, on the eve of his execution, that he "had been happy and still was," and hoped there would be a lot of spectators at the scaffold "to welcome him with cries of hate." "He's a poor fool, an idiot," some people said; others, with greater insight, said, "He's innocent." The meaning of this innocence still remained to be understood.

In *The Myth of Sisyphus*, which appeared a few months later, Camus provided us with a precise commentary upon his work. His hero was neither

From *Literary and Philosophical Essays of Jean-Paul Sartre*. © 1955 Criterion Books Inc.

good nor bad, neither moral nor immoral. These categories do not apply to him. He belongs to a very particular species for which the author reserves the word "absurd." But in Camus's work this word takes on two very different meanings. The absurd is both a state of fact and the lucid awareness which certain people acquire of this state of fact. The "absurd" man is the man who does not hesitate to draw the inevitable conclusions from a fundamental absurdity.

There is the same displacement of meaning as when we give the name "swing" to the youthful generation that dances to "swing" music. What is meant by the absurd as a state of fact, as primary situation? It means nothing less than man's relation to the world. Primary absurdity manifests a cleavage, the cleavage between man's aspirations to unity and the insurmountable dualism of mind and nature, between man's drive toward the eternal and the *finite* character of his existence, between the "concern" which constitutes his very essence and the vanity of his efforts. Chance, death, the irreducible pluralism of life and of truth, the unintelligibility of the real—all these are extremes of the absurd.

These are not really very new themes, and Camus does not present them as such. They had been sounded as early as the seventeenth century by a certain kind of dry, plain, contemplative rationalism, which is typically French and they served as the commonplaces of classical pessimism.

Was it not Pascal who emphasized "the natural misfortune of our mortal and feeble condition, so wretched that when we consider it closely, nothing can console us"? Was it not he who put reason in its place? Would he not have wholeheartedly approved the following remark of Camus: "The world is neither (completely) rational, nor quite irrational either"? Does he not show us that "custom" and "diversion" conceal man's "nothingness, his forlornness, his inadequacy, his impotence and his emptiness" from himself? By virtue of the cool style of *The Myth of Sisyphus* and the subject of his essays, Albert Camus takes his place in the great tradition of those French moralists whom Andler has rightly termed the precursors of Nietzsche.

As to the doubts raised by Camus about the scope of our reasoning powers, these are in the most recent tradition of French epistemology. If we think of scientific nominalism, of Poincaré, Duhem and Meyerson, we are better able to understand the reproach our author addresses to modern science. "You tell me of an invisible planetary system in which electrons revolve about a nucleus. You explain the world to me by means of an image. I then realize that you have ended in poetry . . ." (*The Myth of Sisyphus*). This idea was likewise expressed, and at just about the same time, by another writer, Maurice Merleau-Ponty, who draws on the same material when he says, "Physics uses mechanical, dynamic and even psychological models without any preference, as if, freed of ontological aspirations, it were becoming indifferent to the classical antimonies of the mechanism or dynamism which presupposes a nature-in-itself." (*La Structure du Comportement*). Camus shows off a bit by quoting passages from Jaspers, Heidegger and Kierkegaard, whom, by the way, he does not always seem to have quite understood. But his real masters are to be found elsewhere.

The turn of his reasoning, the clarity of his ideas, the cut of his expository style and a certain kind of solar, ceremonious, and sad sombreness, all indicate a classic temperament, a man of the Mediterranean. His very method ("only through a balance of evidence and lyricism shall we attain a combination of emotion and lucidity.") recalls the old "passionate geometries" of Pascal and Rousseau and relate him, for example, not to a German phenomenologist or a Danish existentialist, but rather to Maurras, that other Mediterranean from whom, however, he differs in many respects.

But Camus would probably be willing to grant all this. To him, originality means pursuing one's ideas to the limit; it certainly does not mean making a collection of pessimistic maxims. The absurd, to be sure, resides neither in man nor in the world, if you consider each separately. But since man's dominant characteristic is "being-in-the-world," the absurd is, in the end, an inseparable part of the human condition. Thus, the absurd is not, to begin with, *the object of a mere idea; it is revealed to us in a doleful illumination.* "Getting up, tram, four hours of work, meal, sleep, and Monday, Tuesday, Wednesday, Thursday, Friday, Saturday, in the same routine" (*Sisyphus*), and then, suddenly, "the setting collapses," and we find ourselves in a state of hopeless lucidity.

If we are able to refuse the misleading aid of religion or of existential philosophies, we then possess certain basic, obvious facts: the world is chaos, a "divine equivalence born of anarchy"; tomorrow does not exist, since we all die. "In a universe suddenly deprived of light and illusions, man feels himself a stranger. This exile is irrevocable, since he has no memories of a lost homeland and no hope of a promised land." The reason is that man is *not* the world.

> If I were a tree among other trees . . . this life would have a meaning, or rather this problem would have none, for I would be part of this world. I *would be* this world against which I set myself with my entire mind. . . . It is preposterous reason which sets me against all creation.

This explains, in part, the title of our novel; the stranger is man confronting the world. Camus might as well have chosen the title of one of George Gissing's works, *Born in Exile*. The stranger is also man among men. "There are days when . . . you find that the person you've loved has become a stranger." The stranger is, finally, myself in relation to myself, that is, natural man in relation to mind: "The stranger who, at certain moments, confronts us in a mirror" (*The Myth of Sisyphus*).

But that is not all; there is a *passion* of the absurd. The absurd man will not commit suicide; he wants to live, without relinquishing any of his certainty, without a future, without hope, without illusion, and without resignation either. He stares at death with passionate attention and this fascination liberates him. He experiences the "divine irresponsibility" of the condemned man.

Since God does not exist and man dies, everything is permissible. One experience is as good as another; the important thing is simply to acquire as many as possible. "The ideal of the absurd man is the present and the succession of present moments before an ever-conscious spirit" (*Sisyphus*). Confronted with this "quantitative ethic" all values collapse; thrown into this world, the absurd man, rebellious and irresponsible, has "nothing to justify." He is *innocent*, innocent as Somerset Maugham's savages before the arrival of the clergyman who teaches them Good and Evil, what is lawful and what is forbidden. For this man, *everything* is lawful. He is as innocent as Prince Mishkin, who "lives in an everlasting present, lightly tinged with smiles and indifference." Innocent in every sense of the word, he, too, is, if you like, an "Idiot."

And now we fully understand the title of Camus's novel. The stranger he wants to portray is precisely one of those terrible innocents who shock society by not accepting the rules of its game. He lives among outsiders, but to them, too, he is a stranger. That is why some people like him—for example, his mistress, Marie, who is fond of him "because he's odd." Others, like the courtroom crowd whose hatred he suddenly feels mounting towards him, hate him for the same reason. And we ourselves, who, on opening the book are not yet familiar with the feeling of the absurd, vainly try to judge him according to our usual standards. For us, too, he is a stranger.

Thus, the shock you felt when you opened the book and read, "I thought that here was another Sunday over with, that Mama was buried now, that I would go back to work again and that, on the whole, nothing had changed," was deliberate. It was the result of your first encounter with the absurd. But you probably hoped that as you progressed your uneasiness would fade, that everything would be slowly clarified, would be given a reasonable justification and explained. Your hopes were disappointed. *The Stranger* is not an explanatory book. The absurd man does not explain; he describes. Nor is it a book which proves anything.

Camus is simply presenting something and is not concerned with a justification of what is fundamentally unjustifiable. *The Myth of Sisyphus* teaches us how to accept our author's novel. In it, we find the theory of the novel of absurdity. Although the absurdity of the human condition is its sole theme, it is not a novel with a message; it does not come out of a "satisfied" kind of thinking, intent on furnishing formal proofs. It is rather the product of a thinking which is "limited, rebellious, and mortal." It is a proof in itself of the futility of abstract reasoning. "The fact that certain great novelists have chosen to write in terms of images rather than of arguments reveals a great deal about a certain kind of thinking common to them all, a conviction of the futility of all explanatory principles, and of the instructive message of sensory impressions" (*The Myth of Sisyphus*).

Thus, the very fact that Camus delivers his message in the form of a novel reveals a proud humility. This is not resignation, but the rebellious recognition of the limitations of human thought. It is true that he felt obliged to make a philosophical translation of his fictional message. *The Myth of Sisyphus* is just that, and we shall see later on how we are to interpret this parallel commentary. But the existence of the translation does not, in any case, alter the gratuitousness of the novel.

The man who creates in absurdity has lost even the illusion of his work's necessity. He wants us, on the contrary, to be constantly aware of its contingent nature. He would like to see, inscribed below it, "might never have been," as Gide wanted "could be continued" written at the end of *The Counterfeiters*. This novel might not have been, like some stone or stream or face. It is a thing in the present that happens, quite simply, like all other happenings in the present. It has not even the subjective necessity that artists pretend to when, speaking of their works, they say, "I had to write it, I had to get it off my chest." In it we find one of the themes of surrealist terrorism sifted through the classic sun. The work of art is only a leaf torn from a life. It does, of course, express this life. But it need not express it. And besides, everything has the same value, whether it be writing *The Possessed* or drinking a cup of coffee.

Camus does not require that attentive solicitude that writers who "have sacrificed their lives to art" demand of the reader, *The Stranger* is a leaf from his life. And since the most absurd life is that which is most sterile, his novel aims at being magnificently sterile. Art is an act of unnecessary generosity. We need not be over-disturbed by this; I find, hidden beneath Camus's paradoxes, some of Kant's wise observations on the "endless end" of the beautiful. Such, in any case, is *The Stranger*, a work detached from a life, unjustified and unjustifiable, sterile, momentary, already forsaken by its author, abandoned for other present things. And that is how we must accept it, as a brief communion between two men, the author and the reader, beyond reason, in the realm of the absurd.

This will give us some idea as to how we are to regard the hero of *The Stranger*. If Camus had wanted to write a novel with a purpose, he would have had no difficulty in showing a civil servant lording it over his family, and then suddenly struck with the intuition of the absurd, struggling against it for a while and finally resolving to live out the fundamental absurdity of his condition. The reader would have been convinced along with the character, and for the same reasons.

Or else, he might have related the life of one of those saints of the Absurd, so dear to his heart, of whom he speaks in *The Myth of Sisyphus*: Don Juan, the Actor, the Conqueror, the Creator. But he has not done so, and Meursault, the hero of *The Stranger*, remains ambiguous, even to the reader who is familiar with theories of the absurd. We are, of course, assured that he is absurd, and his dominant characteristic is a pitiless clarity. Besides, he is, in more ways than one, constructed so as to furnish a concerted illustration of the theories expounded in *The Myth of Sisyphus*. For example, in the latter work, Camus writes, "A man's virility lies more in what he keeps to himself than in what he says." And Meursault is an example of this virile silence, of this refusal to indulge in words: "[He was asked] if he had noticed that I was withdrawn, and he admitted only that I didn't waste words." And two lines before this, the same witness has just declared that Meursault "was a man." "[He was asked] what he meant by that, and he said that everyone knew what he meant."

In like manner Camus expatiates on love in *The Myth of Sisyphus*. "It is only on the basis of a collective way of seeing, for which books and legends are responsible, that we give the name *love* to what binds us to certain human beings." And similarly, we read in *The Stranger*: "So she wanted to know whether I loved her. I answered . . . that it didn't mean anything, but that I probably didn't love her." From this point of view, the debate in the courtroom and in the reader's mind as to whether or not Meursault loved his mother is doubly absurd.

First of all, as the lawyer asks, "Is he accused of having buried his mother or of having killed a man?" But above all, the words "to love" are meaningless. Meursault probably put his mother into an old people's home because he hadn't enough money and because "they had nothing more to say to one another." And he probably did not go to see her often, "because it wasted [his] Sunday—not to speak of the effort involved in getting to the bus, buying tickets, and taking a two-hour trip." But what does this mean? Isn't he living completely in the present, according to his present fancies? What we call a feeling is merely the abstract unity and the meaning of discontinuous impressions.

I am not constantly thinking about the people I love, but I claim to love them even when I am not thinking about them—and I am capable of compromising my well-being in the name of an abstract feeling, in the absence of any real and immediate emotion. Meursault thinks and acts in a different way; he has no desire to know these noble, continuous, completely identical feelings. For him, neither love nor individual loves exist. All that counts is the present and the concrete. He goes to see his mother when he feels like it, and that's that.

If the desire is there, it will be strong enough to make this sluggard run at full speed to jump into a moving truck. But he still calls his mother by the tender, childish name of "Mama," and he never misses a chance to understand her and identify himself with her. "All I know of love is that mixture of desire, tenderness and intelligence that binds me to someone" (*The Myth of Sisyphus*). Thus we see that the *theoretical* side of Meursault's character is not be overlooked. In the same way, many of his adventures are intended chiefly to bring out some aspect or other of the basic absurdity of things. *The Myth of Sisyphus*, for example, extols, as we have seen, the "perfect freedom of the condemned prisoner to whom, some particular daybreak, the prison doors swing open," and it is in order to make us taste this daybreak and freedom that Camus has condemned his hero to capital punishment. "How could I have failed to see," says Meursault, "that nothing was more important than an execution . . . and that it was even, in a way, the only really interesting thing for a man!" One could multiply the examples and quotations.

Nevertheless, this lucid, indifferent, taciturn man is not entirely constructed to serve a cause. Once the character had been sketched in, he probably completed himself; he certainly had a real weight of his own. Still, his absurdity seems to have been given rather than achieved; that's how he is, and that's that. He does have his revelation on the last page, but he has always lived according to Camus's standards. If there were a grace of absurdity, we would have to say that he has grace. He does not seem to pose himself any of the questions explored in *The Myth of Sisyphus*; Meursault is not shown rebelling at his death sentence. He was happy, he has let himself live, and his happiness does not seem to have been marred by that hidden gnawing which Camus frequently mentions in his essay and which is due to the blinding presence of death. His very indifference often seems like indolence, as, for instance, that Sunday when he stays at home out of pure laziness, and when he admits to having been "slightly bored." The character thus retains a real opacity, even to the absurd-conscious observer. He is no Don Juan, no Don Quixote of the absurd; he often even seems like its Sancho Panza. He is there before us, he exists, and we can neither understand nor quite judge him. In a word, he is alive, and all that can justify him to us in his fictional density.

The Stranger is not, however, to be regarded as a completely gratuitous work. Camus distinguishes, as we have mentioned, between the *notion* and the *feeling* of the absurd. He says, in this connection, "Deep feelings, like great works, are always more meaningful than they are aware of being. . . . An intense feeling carries with it its own universe, magnificent or wretched, as the case may be" (*The Myth of Sisyphus*). And he adds, a bit further on, "The feeling of the absurd is not the same as the *idea* of the absurd. The idea is grounded in the feeling, that is all. It does not exhaust it." *The Myth of Sisyphus* might be said to aim at giving us this *idea*, and *The Stranger* at giving us the feeling.

The order in which the two works appeared seems to confirm this hypothesis. *The Stranger*, the first to appear, plunges us without comment into the "climate" of the absurd; the essay then comes and illumines the landscape. Now, absurdity means divorce, discrepancy. *The Stranger* is to be a novel of discrepancy, divorce and disorientation; hence its skillful construction.

We have, on the one hand, the amorphous, everyday flow of reality as it is experienced, and, on the other, the edifying reconstruction of this reality by speech and human reason. The reader, brought face to face with simple reality, must find it again, without being able to recognize it in its rational transposition. This is the source of the feeling of the absurd, that is, of our inability to *think*, with our words and concepts, what happens in the world. Meursault buries his mother, takes a mistress, and commits a crime.

These various facts will be related by witnesses at his trial, and they will be put in order and explained by the public prosecutor. Meursault will have the impression that they are talking of someone else. Everything is so arranged as to bring on the sudden outburst of Marie, who, after giving, in the witness box, an account composed according to human rules, bursts into sobs and says "that that wasn't it, that there was something else, that they were forcing her to say the opposite of what she really thought." These mirror tricks have been used frequently since *The Counterfeiters*, and they do not constitute Camus's originality. But the problem to be solved imposes an original form upon him.

In order to feel the divergence between the prosecutor's conclusions and the actual circumstances of the murder, in order, when we have finished the book, to retain the impression of an absurd justice, incapable of ever understanding or even of making contact with the deeds it intends to punish, we must first have been placed in contact with reality, or with one of these circumstances. But in order to establish this contact, Camus, like the prosecutor, has only words and concepts at his disposal. In assembling thoughts, he is forced to use words to describe a world that precedes words. The first part of *The Stranger* could have been given the same title as a recent book, *Translated from Silence*. Here we touch upon a disease common to many contemporary writers and whose first traces I find in Jules Renard. I shall call it "the obsession with silence." Jean Paulhan would certainly regard it as an effect of literary terrorism.

It has assumed a thousand forms, ranging from the surrealists' automatic writing to Jean-Jacques Bernard's "theatre of silence." The reason is that silence, as Heidegger says, is the authentic mode of speech. Only the man who knows how to talk can be silent. Camus talks a great deal; in *The Myth of Sisyphus* he is even garrulous. And yet, he reveals his love of silence. He quotes Kierkegaard: "The surest way of being mute is not to hold your tongue, but to talk." And he himself adds that "a man is more of a man because of what he does not say than what he does say." Thus, in *The Stranger*, he has attempted *to be silent*. But how is one to be silent with words? How is one to convey through concepts the unthinkable and disorderly succession of present instants? This problem involves resorting to a new technique.

What is this new technique? "It's Kafka written by Hemingway," I was told. I confess that I have found no trace of Kafka in it. Camus's views are entirely of this earth, and Kafka is the novelist of impossible transcendence; for him, the universe is full of signs that we cannot understand; there is a reverse side to the décor. For Camus, on the contrary, the tragedy of human existence lies in the absence of any transcendence.

> I do not know whether this world has a meaning that is beyond me. But I do know that I am unaware of this meaning and that, for the time being, it is impossible for me to know it. What can a meaning beyond my condition mean to me? I can understand only in human terms. I understand the things I touch, things that offer me resistance.

He is not concerned, then, with so ordering words as to suggest an inhuman, indecipherable order; the inhuman is merely the disorderly, the mechanical. There is nothing ambiguous in his work, nothing disquieting, nothing hinted at. *The Stranger* gives us a succession of luminously clear views. If they bewilder us, it is only because of their number and the absence of any link between them. Camus likes bright mornings, clear evenings, and relentless afternoons. His favorite season is Algiers' eternal summer. Night has hardly any place in his universe.

When he does talk of it, it is in the following terms: "I awakened with stars about my face. Country noises reached my ears. My temples were soothed by odors of night, earth, and salt. The wonderful peace of that sleepy summer invaded me like a tide" (*The Stranger*). The man who wrote these lines is as far removed as possible from the anguish of a Kafka. He is very much at peace within disorder. Nature's obstinate blindness probably irritates him, but it comforts him as well. Its irrationality is only a negative thing. The absurd man is a humanist; he knows only the good things of this world.

The comparison with Hemingway seems more fruitful. The relationship between the two styles is obvious. Both men write in the same short sentences. Each sentence refuses to exploit the momentum accumulated by preceding ones. Each is a new beginning. Each is like a snapshot of a gesture or object. For each new gesture and word there is a new and corresponding sentence. Nevertheless, I am not quite satisfied. The existence of an "American" narrative technique has certainly been of help to Camus. I doubt whether it has, strictly speaking, influenced him.

Even in *Death in the Afternoon*, which is not a novel, Hemingway retains that abrupt style of narration that shoots each separate sentence out of the void with a sort of respiratory spasm. His style is himself. We know that Camus has another style, a ceremonious one. But even in *The Stranger* he occasionally heightens the tone. His sentences then take on a larger, more continuous, movement.

> The cry of the news-vendors in the relaxed air, the last birds in the square, the calls of the sandwich-vendors, the wail of the trams on the high curves of the city and the distant murmur in the sky before night began to teeter over the port, all set before me a blind man's route with which I was familiar long before entering prison.

Through the transparency of Meursault's breathless account I catch a glimpse of a poetic prose underneath, which is probably Camus's personal mode of expression. If *The Stranger* exhibits such visible traces of the American technique, it was deliberate on Camus's part. He has chosen from among all the instruments at his disposal the one which seemed to serve his purpose best. I doubt whether he will use it again in future works.

Let us examine the plot a little more closely; we shall get a clearer notion of the author's methods. "Men also secrete the inhuman," writes Camus. "Sometimes, in moments of lucidity, the mechanical aspect of their gestures and their senseless pantomime make everything about them seem stupid" (*The Myth of Sisyphus*). This quality must be rendered at once. *The Stranger* must put us right from the start "into a state of uneasiness when confronted with man's inhumanity."

But what are the particular occasions that create this uneasiness in us? *The Myth of Sisyphus* gives us an example. "A man is talking on the telephone. We cannot hear him behind the glass partition, but we can see his senseless mimicry. We wonder why he is alive?" This answers the question almost too well, for the example reveals a certain bias in the author. The gesturing of a man who is telephoning and whom we cannot hear is really only *relatively* absurd, because it is part of an incomplete circuit. Listen in on an extension, however, and the circuit is completed; human activity recovers its meaning. Therefore, one would have, in all honesty, to admit that there are only relative absurdities and only in relation to "absolute rationalities."

However, we are not concerned with honesty, but with art. Camus has a method ready to hand. He is going to insert a glass partition between the reader and his characters. Is there really anything sillier than a man behind a glass window? Glass seems to let everything through. It stops only one thing: the meaning of his gestures. The glass remains to be chosen. It will be the Stranger's mind, which is really transparent, since we see everything it sees. However, it is so constructed as to be transparent to things and opaque to meanings.

> From then on, everything went very quickly. The men went up to the coffin with a sheet. The priest, his followers, the director and I, all went outside. In front of the door was a lady I didn't know. "Monsieur Meursault," said the director. I didn't hear the lady's name, and I gathered only that she was a nurse who'd been ordered to be present. Without smiling, she nodded her long, bony face. Then we stood aside to make room for the body to pass. (*The Stranger*)

Some men are dancing behind a glass partition. Between them and the reader has been interposed a consciousness, something very slight, a translucent curtain, a pure passivity that merely records all the facts. But it has done the trick. Just because it is passive, this consciousness records only facts. The reader has not noticed this presence. But what is the assumption implied by this kind of narrative technique? To put it briefly, what had once been melodic structure has been transformed into a sum of invariant elements. This succession of *movements* is supposed to be rigorously identical with the *act* considered as a complete entity. Are we not dealing here with the analytic assumption that any reality is reducible to a sum total of elements? Now, though analysis may be the instrument of science, it is also the instrument of humor. If in describing a rugby match, I write, "I saw adults in shorts fighting and throwing themselves on the ground in order to send a leather ball between a pair of wooden posts," I have summed up what I have *seen*, but I have intentionally missed its meaning. I am merely trying to be humorous. Camus's story is analytic and humorous. Like all artists, he *invents*, because

he pretends to be reconstituting raw experience and because he slyly elimi-
nates all the significant links which are also part of the experience.

That is what Hume did when he stated that he could find nothing in
experience but isolated impressions. That is what the American neorealists
still do when they deny the existence of any but external relations between
phenomena. Contemporary philosophy has, however, established the fact
that meanings are also part of the immediate data. But this would carry us
too far afield. We shall simply indicate that the universe of the absurd man is
the analytic world of the neo-realists. In literature, this method has proved
its worth. It was Voltaire's method in *L'Ingénu* and *Micromégas*, and Swift's in
Gulliver's Travels. For the eighteenth century also had its own outsiders,
"noble savages," usually, who, transported to a strange civilization, perceived
facts before being able to grasp their meaning. The effect of this discrepancy
was to arouse in the reader the feeling of the absurd. Camus seems to have
this in mind on several occasions, particularly when he shows his hero
reflecting on the reasons for his imprisonment.

It is this analytic process that explains the use of the American technique in *The Stranger*. The presence of death at the end of our path has made
our future go up in smoke; our life has "no future"; it is a series of present
moments. What does this mean, if not that the absurd man is applying his
analytical spirit to Time? Where Bergson saw an indestructible organization,
he sees only a series of instants. It is the plurality of incommunicable
moments that will finally account for the plurality of beings. What our
author borrows from Hemingway is thus the discontinuity between the
clipped phrases that imitate the discontinuity of time.

We are now in a better position to understand the form of his narrative. Each sentence is a present instant, but not an indecisive one that spreads
like a stain to the following one. The sentence is sharp, distinct, and self-
contained. It is separated by a void from the following one, just as Descartes's
instant is separated from the one that follows it. The world is destroyed and
reborn from sentence to sentence. When the word makes its appearance it is
a creation *ex nihilo*. The sentences in *The Stranger* are islands. We bounce
from sentence to sentence, from void to void. It was in order to emphasize
the isolation of each sentence unit that Camus chose to tell his story in the
present perfect tense. The simple past is the tense of continuity: "*Il se
promena longtemps.*" These words refer us to a past perfect, to a future. The
reality of the sentence is the verb, the act, with its transitive character and its
transcendence. "*Il s'est promené longtemps*" conceals the verbality of the verb.
The verb is split and broken in two.

On the one hand, we find a past participle which has lost all transcendence and which is as inert as a thing; and on the other, we find only the verb

être, which has merely a copulative sense and which joins the participle to the substantive as the attribute to the subject. The transitive character of the verb has vanished; the sentence has frozen. Its present reality becomes the noun. Instead of acting as a bridge between past and future, it is merely a small, isolated, self-sufficient substance.

If, in addition, you are careful to reduce it as much as possible to the main proposition, its internal structure attains a perfect simplicity. It gains thereby in cohesiveness. It becomes truly indivisible, an atom of time. The sentences are not, of course, arranged in relation to each other; they are simply juxtaposed. In particular, all causal links are avoided lest they introduce the germ of an explanation and an order other than that of pure succession. Consider the following passage:

> She asked me, a moment later, if I loved her. *I answered that it didn't mean anything, but that I probably didn't love her. She seemed sad.* But while preparing lunch, for no reason at all she suddenly laughed in such a way that I kissed her. Just then, the noise of an argument broke out at Raymond's place.

I have cited two sentences which most carefully conceal the causal link under the simple appearance of succession.

When it is absolutely necessary to allude to a preceding sentence, the author uses words like "and," "but," "then," and "just then," which evoke only disjunction, opposition, or mere addition. The relations between these temporal units, like those established between objects by the neo-realists, are external. Reality appears on the scene without being introduced and then disappears without being destroyed. The world dissolves and is reborn with each pulsation of time. But we must not think it is self-generated. Any activity on its part would lead to a substitution by dangerous forces for the reassuring disorder of pure chance.

A nineteenth-century naturalist would have written, "A bridge spanned the river." Camus will have none of this anthropomorphism. He says "Over the river was a bridge." This object thus immediately betrays its passiveness. It *is there* before us, plain and undifferentiated. "There were four negro men in the room . . . in front of the door was a lady I didn't know. . . . Beside her was the director. . . ." People used to say that Jules Renard would end by writing things like "The hen lays." Camus and many other contemporary writers would write "There is the hen and she lays." The reason is that they like things for their own sake and do not want to dilute them in the flux of duration. "There is water." Here we have a bit of eternity—passive, impenetrable, incommunicable and gleaming! What sensual delight, if only we could touch it! To the absurd man, this is the one and only good. And that is why the novelist prefers these short-lived little sparkles, each of which gives a bit of pleasure, to an organized narrative.

This is what enables Camus to think that in writing *The Stranger* he remains silent. His sentence does not belong to the universe of discourse. It has neither ramifications nor extensions nor internal structure. It might be defined, like Valéry's sylph, as

> Neither seen nor known:
> The time of a bare breast
> Between two shifts.

It is very exactly measured by the time of a silent intuition. If this is so, can we speak of Camus's novel as something whole? All the sentences of his book are equal to each other, just as all the absurd man's experiences are equal. Each one sets up for itself and sweeps the others into the void. But, as a result, no single one of them detaches itself from the background of the others, except for the rare moments in which the author, abandoning these principles, becomes poetic.

The very dialogues are integrated into the narrative. Dialogue is the moment of explanation, of meaning, and to give it a place of honor would be to admit that meanings exist. Camus irons out the dialogue, summarizes it, renders it frequently as indirect discourse. He denies it any typographic privileges, so that a spoken phrase seems like any other happening. It flashes for an instant and then disappears, like heat lightning. Thus, when you start reading the book you feel as if you were listening to a monotonous, nasal, Arab chant rather than reading a novel. You may think that the novel is going to be like one of those tunes of which Courteline remarked that "they disappear, never to return" and stop all of a sudden. But the work gradually organizes itself before the reader's eyes and reveals its solid substructure.

There is not a single unnecessary detail, not one that is not returned to later on and used in the argument. And when we close the book, we realize that it could not have had any other ending. In this world that has been stripped of its causality and presented as absurd, the smallest incident has weight. There is no single one which does not help to lead the hero to crime and capital punishment. *The Stranger* is a classical work, an orderly work, composed about the absurd and against the absurd. Is this quite what the author was aiming at? I do not know. I am simply presenting the reader's opinion.

How are we to classify this clear, dry work, so carefully composed beneath its seeming disorder, so "human," so open, too, once you have the key? It cannot be called a *récit*, for a *récit* explains and co-ordinates as it narrates. It substitutes the order of causality for chronological sequence. Camus calls it a "novel." The novel, however, requires continuous duration, development and the manifest presence of the irreversibility of time. I would hesitate somewhat to use the term "novel" for this succession of inert present moments which allows us to see, from underneath, the mechanical economy of something deliberately staged. Or, if it is a novel, it is so in the sense that *Zadig* and *Candide* are novels. It might be regarded as a moralist's short novel, one with a discreet touch of satire and a series of ironic portraits (those of the pimp, the judge, the prosecuting attorney, etc.), a novel that, for all the influence of the German existentialists and the American novelists, remains, at bottom, very close to the tales of Voltaire.

ALBERT CAMUS

Preface to the American Edition of The Stranger

I summarized *The Stranger* a long time ago, with a remark that I admit was highly paradoxical: "In our society any man who does not weep at his mother's funeral runs the risk of being sentenced to death." I only meant that the hero of my book is condemned because he does not play the game. In this respect, he is foreign to the society in which he lives; he wanders, on the fringe, in the suburbs of private, solitary, sensual life. And this is why some readers have been tempted to look upon him as a piece of social wreckage. A much more accurate idea of the character, or, at least one much closer to the author's intentions, will emerge if one asks just *how* Meursault doesn't play the game. The reply is a simple one: he refuses to lie. To lie is not only to say what isn't true. It is also and above all, to say *more* than is true, and, as far as the human heart is concerned, to express more than one feels. This is what we all do, every day, to simplify life. He says what he is, he refuses to hide his feelings, and immediately society feels threatened. He is asked, for example, to say that he regrets his crime, in the approved manner. He replies that what he feels is annoyance rather than real regret. And this shade of meaning condemns him.

For me, therefore, Meursault is not a piece of social wreckage, but a poor and naked man enamored of a sun that leaves no shadows. Far from being bereft of all feelings, he is animated by a passion that is deep because it is stubborn, a passion for the absolute and for truth. This truth is still a negative one, the truth of what we are and what we feel, but without it no conquest of ourselves or of the world will ever be possible.

One would therefore not be much mistaken to read *The Stranger* as the story of a man who, without any heroics, agrees to die for the truth. I also happened to say, again paradoxically, that I had tried to draw in my character the only Christ we deserve. It will be understood, after my explanations, that I said this with no blasphemous intent, and only with the slightly ironic affection an artist has the right to feel for the characters he has created.

ALAIN ROBBE-GRILLET

Nature, Humanism, Tragedy

> Tragedy is merely a means of "recovering"
> human misery, of subsuming and thereby justi-
> fying it in the form of a necessity, a wisdom, or a
> purification: to refuse this recuperation and to
> investigate the techniques of not treacherously
> succumbing to it (nothing is more insidious than
> tragedy) is today a necessary enterprise.
> —Roland Barthes

As recently as two years ago, trying to define the direction of a still tenta-
tive development in the art of the novel, I described as a constant factor "the
destitution of the old myths of depth." The violent and almost unanimous
reactions of the critics, the objections of many readers of apparent good
faith, the reservations formulated by several sincere friends have persuaded
me that I went too far too fast. Apart from several men themselves engaged
in comparable investigations—artistic, literary, or philosophical—no one
would grant that such an assertion did not necessarily involve the negation
of Man himself. Loyalty to the old myths showed itself to be, as matter of
fact, quite tenacious.

That writers as different as François Mauriac and André Rousseaux, for
example, should concur in denouncing the exclusive description of "surfaces"

From *For a New Novel: Essays on Fiction.* © 1965 by Grove Press, Inc.

as a gratuitous mutilation, the blind folly of a young rebel, a kind of sterile despair leading to the destruction of art nonetheless seemed quite in order. More unexpected, more disturbing, was the position—identical, from many points of view—of certain materialists who, in order to judge my enterprise, referred to "values" remarkably similar to the traditional values of Christianity. Yet for them there was no question of a confessional *parti pris*. But on either side, what was offered as a principle was the indefectible solidarity between our mind and the world, while art was reduced to its "natural," reassuring role as mediator; and I was condemned in the name of the "human."

Finally I was quite naive, it was said, to attempt to deny this depth: my own books were interesting, were readable, only to the degree—and the degree was disputed—to which they were, unknown to me, its expression.

That there is no more than a rather loose parallelism between the three novels I have published up to now and my theoretical views on a possible novel of the future is certainly obvious enough. Moreover, it will be regarded as only natural that a book of two or three hundred pages should be more complex than an article of ten; and also, that it is easier to indicate a new direction than to follow it, without failure—partial or even complete—being a decisive, definitive proof of the error committed at the outset.

Finally, it must be added that the characteristic of humanism, whether Christian or not, is precisely to recover *everything*, including whatever attempts to trace its limits, even to impugn it as a whole. This is, in fact, one of the surest resources of its functioning.

There is no question of seeking to justify myself at any price; I am merely trying to see the matter more clearly. The critical positions cited above help me do so in a notable way. What I am undertaking today is less to refute their arguments than to define their scope, and to define at the same time what separates me from such points of view. It is always futile to engage in polemics; but if a true dialogue is possible, one must on the contrary seize the opportunity to engage in it. And if dialogue is not possible, it is important to know why. In any case, we are doubtless all, on one side as on the other, interested enough in these problems to make it worth while discussing them again, however bluntly.

Is there not, first of all, a certain fraudulence in this word *human* which is always being thrown in our faces? If it is not a word quite devoid of meaning, what meaning does it really have?

It seems that those who use it all the time, those who make it the sole criterion of all praise as of all reproach, identify—deliberately, perhaps—a precise (and limited) reflection on man, his situation in the world, the phenomena of his existence, with a certain anthropocentric atmosphere, vague but imbuing all things, giving the world its so-called *signification*, that is, investing it from within by a more or less disingenuous network of sentiments and thoughts. Simplifying, we can summarize the position of our new inquisitors in two sentences; if I say, "The world is man," I shall always gain absolution; while if I say, "Things are things, and man is only man," I am immediately charged with a crime against humanity.

The crime is the assertion that there exists something in the world which is not man, which makes no sign to him, which has nothing in common with him. The crime, above all, according to this view, is to remark this separation, this distance, without attempting to effect the slightest sublimation of it.

What could be, in other words, an "inhuman" work? How, in particular, could a novel which deals with a man, and follows his steps from page to page, describing only what he does, what he sees, or what he imagines, how could such a novel be accused of turning away from man? And it is not the character himself, let us make that clear at once, who is involved in this judgment. As a "character," as an individual animated by torments and passions, no one will ever reproach him with being inhuman, even if he is a sadistic madman and a criminal—the contrary, it would seem.

But now suppose the eyes of this man rest on things without indulgence, insistently: he sees them, but he refuses to appropriate them, he refuses to maintain any suspect understanding with them, any complicity; he asks nothing of them; toward them he feels neither agreement nor dissent of any kind. He can, perhaps, make them the prop of his passions, as of his sense of sight. But his sense of sight is content to take their measurements; and his passion, similarly, rests on their surface, without attempting to penetrate them since there is nothing inside, without feigning the least appeal since they would not answer.

To condemn, in the name of the human, the novel which deals with such a man is therefore to adopt the *humanist* point of view, according to which it is not enough to show man where he is: it must further be proclaimed that man is everywhere. On the pretext that man can achieve only a subjective knowledge of the world, humanism decides to elect man the justification of everything. A true bridge of souls thrown between man and things, the humanist outlook is preeminently a pledge of solidarity.

In the literary realm, the expression of this solidarity appears chiefly as the investigation, worked up into a system, of analogical relations.

Metaphor, as a matter of fact, is never an innocent figure of speech. To say that the weather is "capricious" or the mountain "majestic," to speak of the "heart" of the forest, of a "pitiless" sun, of a village "huddled" in the valley, is, to a certain degree, to furnish clues as to the things themselves:

/

shape, size, situation, etc. But the choice of an analogical vocabulary, however simple, already does something more than account for purely physical data, and what this *more* is can scarcely be ascribed only to the credit of belles-lettres. The height of the mountain assumes, willy-nilly, a moral value; the heat of the sun becomes the result of an intention. . . . In almost the whole of our contemporary literature, these anthropomorphic analogies are repeated too insistently, too coherently not to reveal an entire metaphysical system.

More or less consciously, the goal for the writers who employ such a terminology can only be to establish a constant relation between the universe and the being who inhabits it. Thus man's sentiments will seem alternately to derive from his contacts with the world and to find in that world their natural correspondence if not their fulfillment.

Metaphor, which is supposed to express only a comparison, without any particular motive, actually introduces a subterranean communication, a movement of sympathy (or of antipathy) which is its true *raison d'être*. For, as comparison, metaphor is almost always a useless comparison which contributes nothing new to the description. What would the village lose by being merely "situated" in the valley? The word "huddled" gives us no complementary information. On the other hand it transports the reader (in the author's wake) into the imagined soul of the village; if I accept the word "huddled," I am no longer entirely a spectator; I myself become the village, for the duration of a sentence, and the valley functions as a cavity into which I aspire to disappear.

Taking this possible adherence as their basis, the defenders of metaphor reply that it thereby possesses an advantage: that of making apparent an element which was not so. Having himself become the village, they say, the reader participates in the latter's situation, hence understands it better. Similarly in the case of the mountain: I shall make it easier to see the mountain by saying it is majestic than by measuring the apparent angle from which my gaze registers its height. . . . And this is true sometimes, but it always involves a more serious reversal: it is precisely this participation which is problematical, since it leads to the notion of a hidden unity.

It must even be added that the gain in descriptive value is here no more than an alibi: the true lovers of metaphor seek only to impose the idea of a communication. If they did not possess the verb "huddle," they would not even mention the position of the village. The height of the mountain would be nothing to them, if it did not offer the moral spectacle of "majesty."

Such a spectacle, for them, never remains entirely *external*. It always implies, more or less, a gift received by man: the things around him are like the fairies in the tale, each of whom brought as a gift to the newborn child one of the traits of his future character. The mountain might thus have first communicated to me the feeling of the majestic—that is what is insinuated. This feeling would then be developed in me and, by a natural growth, engender others: magnificence, prestige, heroism, nobility, pride. In my turn I would refer these to other objects, even those of a lesser size (I would speak of a proud oak, of a vase of noble lines), and the world would become the depository of all my aspirations to greatness, would be both their image and their justification, for all eternity.

The same would be true of every feeling, and in these incessant exchanges, multiplied to infinity, I could no longer discern the origin of anything. Was majesty to be located first within, or around me? The question itself would lose its meaning. Only a sublime communion would remain between the world and me.

Then, with habit, I would easily go much farther. Once the principle of this communion was admitted, I would speak of the melancholy of a landscape, of the indifference of a stone, of the fatuousness of a coal scuttle. These new metaphors no longer furnish appreciable information about the objects subject to my scrutiny, but the world of things has been so thoroughly contaminated by my mind that it is henceforth susceptible of any emotion, of any character trait. I will forget that it is I, I alone, who feels melancholy or suffers solitude; these affective elements will soon be considered as the *profound reality* of the material universe, the sole reality—to all intents and purposes—worthy of engaging my interest in it.

Hence there is much more involved than describing our consciousness by using things as raw material, as one might build a cabin out of logs. To identify in this way my own melancholy with that which I attribute to a landscape, to admit this link as more than superficial, is thereby to acknowledge a certain predestination for my present life: this landscape existed *before* me; if it is really the landscape which is sad, it was *already* sad before me, and this correspondence I experience today between its form and my mood were here waiting for me long before I was born; this melancholy has been fated for me forever. . . .

We see to what point the idea of a human *nature* can be linked to the analogical vocabulary. This nature, common to all men, eternal and inalienable, no longer requires a God to establish it. It is enough to know that Mont Blanc has been waiting for me in the heart of the Alps since the tertiary era, and with it all my notions of greatness and purity!

This nature, moreover, does not merely belong to man, since it constitutes the link between his mind and things: it is, in fact, an essence common to all "creation" that we are asked to believe in. The universe and I now have only one soul, only one secret.

Belief in a *nature* thus reveals itself as the source of all humanism, in the habitual sense of the word. And it is no accident if Nature precisely—mineral, animal, vegetable Nature—is first of all clogged with an anthropomorphic vocabulary. This Nature—mountain, sea, forest, desert, valley—is simultaneously our model and our heart. It is, at the same time, within us and around us. It is neither provisional nor contingent. It encrusts us, judges us, and ensures our salvation.

To reject our so-called "nature" and the vocabulary which perpetuates its myth, to propose objects as purely external and superficial, is not—as has been claimed—to deny man: but it is to reject the "pananthropic" notion contained in traditional humanism, and probably in all humanism. It is no more in the last analysis than to lay claim, quite logically, to my freedom.

Therefore nothing must be neglected in this mopping-up operation. Taking a closer look, we realize that the anthropocentric analogies (mental or visceral) are not the only ones to be arraigned. *All* analogies are just as dangerous. And perhaps the most dangerous ones of all are the most secret, those in which man is not named.

Let us give some examples, at random. To discover the shape of a horse in the heavens may, of course, derive from a simple process of description and not be of any consequence. But to speak of the "gallop" of the clouds, or of their "flying mane," is no longer entirely innocent. For if a cloud (or a wave or a hill) possesses a mane, if later on the mane of a stallion "flings arrows," if the arrow . . . etc., the reader of such images will emerge from the universe of forms to find himself plunged into a universe of significations. Between the wave and the horse, he will be tempted to conceive an undifferentiated profundity: passion, pride, power, wildness. . . . The idea of a nature leads infallibly to that of a nature common to all things, that is, a *superior* or *higher* nature. The idea of an interiority always leads to the idea of a transcendence.

And the task extends step by step: from the bow to the horse, from the horse to the wave—and from the sea to love. A common nature, once again, must be the eternal answer to the *single question* of our Greco-Christian civilization; the Sphinx is before me, questions me, I need not even try to understand the terms of the riddle being asked, there is only one answer possible, only one answer to everything: man.

This will not do.

There are *questions*, and *answers*. Man is merely, from his own point of view, the only witness.

Man looks at the world, and the world does not look back at him. Man sees things and discovers, now, that he can escape the metaphysical pact others had once concluded for him, and thereby escape servitude and terror. That he can . . . that he *may*, at least, some day.

He does not thereby refuse all contact with the world; he consents on the contrary to utilize it for material ends: a utensil, *as* a utensil, never possesses "depth"; a utensil is entirely form and matter—and purpose.

Man grasps his hammer (or a stone he has selected) and pounds on a stake he wants to drive into the ground. While he uses it in this way, the hammer (or the stone) is merely form and substance: its weight, the striking surface, the other extremity which allows him to hold it. Afterward, man sets the tool down in front of him; if he no longer needs it, the hammer is no more than a thing among things: outside of his use, it has no signification.

And man today (or tomorrow) no longer experiences this absence of signification as a lack, or as a laceration. Confronting such a void, he henceforth feels no dizziness. His heart no longer needs an abyss in which to lodge.

For if he rejects communion, he also rejects tragedy.

Tragedy may be defined, here, as an attempt to "recover" the distance which exists between man and things as a new value; it would be then a test, an ordeal in which victory would consist in being vanquished. Tragedy therefore appears as the last invention of humanism to permit nothing to escape: since the correspondence between man and things has finally been denounced, the humanist saves his empire by immediately instituting a new form of solidarity, the divorce itself becoming a major path to redemption.

There is still almost a communion, but a *painful* one, perpetually in doubt and always deferred, its effectiveness in proportion to its inaccessible character. Divorce-as-a-form-of-marriage is a trap—and it is a falsification.

We see in effect to what degree such a union is perverted: instead of being the quest for a good, it is now the benediction of an evil. Unhappiness, failure, solitude, guilt, madness—such are the accidents of our existence which we are asked to entertain as the best pledges of our salvation. To entertain, not to accept: it is a matter of feeding them at our expense while continuing to struggle against them. For tragedy involves neither a true acceptance nor a true rejection. It is the sublimation of a difference.

Let us retrace, as an example, the functioning of "solitude." I call out. No one answers me. Instead of concluding that there is no one there—which could be a pure and simple observation, dated and localized in space and time—I decide to act as if there *were* someone there, but someone who, for one reason or another, will not answer. The silence which follows my outcry is henceforth no longer a *true* silence; it is charged with a content, a meaning, a depth, a soul—which immediately sends me back to my own. The distance between my cry, to my own ears, and the mute (perhaps deaf) interlocutor to whom it is addressed becomes an anguish, my hope and my despair, a meaning in my life. Henceforth nothing will matter except this false void and the problems it raises for me. Should I call any longer? Should I shout louder? Should I utter different words? I try once again. . . . Very quickly I realize that no one will answer; but the invisible presence I continue to create by my call obliges me to hurl my wretched cries into the silence forever. Soon the sound they make begins to stupefy me. As though bewitched, I call again . . . and again. My solitude, aggravated, is ultimately transmuted into a superior necessity for my alienated consciousness, a promise of my redemption. And I am obliged, if this redemption is to be fulfilled, to persist until my death, crying out for nothing.

According to the habitual process, my solitude is then no longer an accidental, momentary datum of my existence. It becomes part of me, of the entire world, of all men: it is our nature, once again. It is a solitude forever.

Wherever there is distance, separation, doubling, cleavage, there is the possibility of experiencing them as suffering, then of raising this suffering to the height of a sublime necessity. A path toward a metaphysical Beyond, this pseudo-necessity is at the same time the closed door to a realistic future. Tragedy, if it consoles us today, forbids any solider conquest tomorrow. Under the appearance of a perpetual motion, it actually petrifies the universe in a sonorous malediction. There can no longer be any question of seeking some remedy for our misfortune, once tragedy convinces us to love it.

We are in the presence of an oblique maneuver of contemporary humanism, which may deceive us. Since the effort of recuperation no longer bears on things themselves, we might suppose, at first sight, that the divorce between them and man is in any case consummated. But we soon realize that nothing of the kind is the case: whether the pact is concluded with things or with their distance from us comes down to the same thing; the "bridge of souls" subsists between them and us; in fact it is actually reinforced from the operation.

This is why the tragic sense of life never seeks to suppress the distances: it multiplies them, on the contrary, at will. Distance between man and other men, distance between man and himself, between man and the world, between the world and itself—nothing remains intact: everything is lacerated, fissured, divided, displaced. Within the most homogeneous objects as in the least ambiguous situations appears a kind of secret distance. But this is precisely an *interior distance*, a false distance, which is in reality as well-marked path, that is, already a reconciliation.

Everything is contaminated. It seems, though, that the favorite domain of tragedy is the narrative complication, the romanesque. From all mistresses-turned-nuns to all detective-gangsters, by way of all tormented criminals, all pure-souled prostitutes, all the just men constrained by conscience to injustice, all the sadists driven by love, all the madmen pursued by logic, a good "character" in a novel must above all be *double*. The plot will be "human" in proportion to its *ambiguity*. Finally the whole book will be true in proportion to its contradictions.

It is easy to ridicule. It is less so to free oneself from the tragic conditioning our mental civilization imposes upon us. One might even say that the rejection of the ideas of "nature" and of predestination lead *first* to tragedy. There is no important work in contemporary literature that does not contain at the same time the assertion of our freedom and the "tragic" germ of its abandonment.

Two great works at least, in recent decades, have offered us two new forms of the fatal complicity: absurdity and nausea.

Albert Camus, as we know, has named *absurdity* the impassable gulf which exists between man and the world, between the aspirations of the human mind and the world's incapacity to satisfy them. Absurdity is in neither man nor things, but in the impossibility of establishing between them any relation other than *strangeness*.

Every reader has noticed, nonetheless, that the hero of *The Stranger* maintains an obscure complicity with the world, composed of rancor and fascination. The relations of this man with the objects surrounding him are not at all innocent: absurdity constantly involves disappointment, withdrawal, rebellion. It is no exaggeration to claim that it is things, quite specifically, which ultimately lead this man to crime: the sun, the sea, the brilliant sand, the gleaming knife, the spring among the rocks, the revolver. . . . As, of course, among these things, the leading role is taken by Nature.

Thus the book is not written in a language as *filtered* as the first pages may lead one to believe. Only, in fact, the objects already charged with a flagrant human content are carefully neutralized, and *for moral reasons* (such as the old mother's coffin, whose screws are described in terms of their shape and the depth they penetrate into the wood). Alongside this we discover, increasingly numerous as the moment of the murder approaches, the most revealing classical metaphors, naming man or infected by his omnipresence: the countryside is "swollen with sunlight," the evening is "like a melancholy truce," the rutted road reveals the "shiny flesh" of the tar, the soil is "the color of blood," the sun is a "blinding rain," its reflection on a shell is "a sword of light," the day has "cast anchor in an ocean of molten metal"—not to mention the "breathing" of the "lazy" waves, the "somnolent" headland, the sea that "pants" and the "cymbals" of the sun. . . .

The crucial scene of the novel affords the perfect image of a painful solidarity: the implacable sun is always "the same," its reflection on the blade of the knife the Arab is holding "strikes" the hero full in the face and "searches" his eyes, his hand tightens on the revolver, he tries to "shake off" the sun, he fires again, four times. "And it was—he says—as though I had knocked four times on the door of unhappiness."

Absurdity, then, is really a form of tragic humanism. It is not an observation of the separation between man and things. It is a lover's quarrel, which leads to a crime of passion. The world is accused of complicity in a murder.

When Sartre writes (in *Situations I*) that *The Stranger* "rejects anthropomorphism," he is giving us, as the quotations above show, an incomplete view of the work. Sartre has doubtless noticed these passages, but he supposes that Camus, "unfaithful to his principle, is being poetic." Can we not say, rather, that these metaphors are precisely the explanation of the book? Camus does not reject anthropomorphism, he utilizes it with economy and subtlety in order to give it more weight.

Everything is in order, since the point is ultimately, as Sartre points out, to show us, according to Pascal's phrase "the natural unhappiness of our condition."

And what does *Nausea* offer us? It is evidently concerned with strictly visceral relations with the world, dismissing any effort of description (called futile) in favor of a suspect intimacy, presented moreover as illusory, but which the narrator does not imagine he can avoid yielding to. The important thing, in his eyes, is in fact to yield to it as much as possible, in order to arrive at self-awareness.

It is significant that the three first perceptions recorded at the beginning of the book are all gained by the sense of touch, not that of sight. The three objects which provoke revelation are, in effect, respectively, the pebble on the beach, the bolt of a door, the hand of the Self-Taught Man. Each time, it is the physical contact with the narrator's hand which provokes the shock. We know that the sense of touch constitutes, in everyday life, a much more *intimate* sensation than that of sight: no one is afraid of contracting a contagious disease merely by looking at a sick man. The sense of smell is even more suspect: it implies a penetration of the body by the alien thing. The domain of sight itself, moreover, involves different qualities of apprehension: a shape, for example, will generally be more certain than a color, which changes with the light, with the background accompanying it, with the subject considering it.

Hence we are not surprised to note that the eyes of Roquentin, the hero of *Nausea*, are more attracted by colors—particularly by the less determined shades—than by outlines; when it is not his sense of touch, it is almost always the sight of an ill-defined color which provokes the nausea. We recall the importance assumed, at the beginning of the book, by Cousin Adolphe's suspenders, which are scarcely visible against the blue of his shirt: they are "mauve . . . buried in the blue, but with false humility . . . as if, having started out to become violet, they had stopped on the way without abandoning their pretensions. One feels like telling them: 'Go on, *become* violet and get it over with.' But no, they remain in suspension, checked by their incompleted effort. Sometimes the blue that surrounds them slides over them and covers them completely: I remain without seeing them for a moment. But this is only a transition, soon the blue pales in places, and I see patches of the hesitant mauve reappearing, which spread, connect, and reconstitute the suspenders." And the reader will continue to be ignorant of the suspenders' shape. Later, in the park, the famous root of the chestnut tree finally concentrates all its absurdity and its hypocrisy in its black color: "Black? I felt the word draining, emptying out its meaning with an extraordinary rapidity. Black? The root *was not* black, *that* wasn't black there on that piece of wood . . . but rather the vague effort to *imagine black* on the part of someone who had never seen it and who could not have decided on it, who would have imagined an ambiguous being, beyond colors." And Roquentin comments on himself: "Colors, tastes, smells were never real, never truly themselves and nothing but themselves."

As a matter of fact, colors afford him sensations analogous to those of the sense of touch: they are for him an appeal, immediately followed by a withdrawal, then another appeal, etc.; this is a "suspect" contact accompanied by unnameable impressions, demanding an adherence and rejecting it at the same time. Color has the same effect on his eyes as a physical presence on the palm of his hand: it manifests above all an indiscreet (and, of course, double) "personality" of the object, a kind of shameful insistence which is simultaneously complaint, challenge, and denial. "Objects . . . they touch me, it's unbearable. I'm afraid of entering into contact with them, just as if they were living creatures." Color changes, hence it is *alive*; that is what Roquentin has discovered: things are alive, *like himself*.

Sounds seem to him similarly corrupted (aside from musical tunes, which do not *exist*). There remains the visual perception of outlines; we feel that Roquentin avoids attacking these. Yet he rejects in turn this last refuge of coincidence with himself: the only lines which coincide exactly are geometric lines, the circles for example, "but the circle too does not exist."

We are, once again, in an entirely *tragedified* universe: fascination with doubling, solidarity with things *because* they bear their own negation within themselves, redemption (here: accession to consciousness) by the very impossibility of achieving a true correspondence; in other words, the final recuperation of all distances, of all failures, of all solitudes, of all contradictions.

Hence analogy is the only mode of description seriously envisaged by Roquentin. Facing the cardboard box containing his bottle of ink, he discovers the futility of geometry in this realm: to say that it is a paral-lelepiped is to say nothing at all "about it." On the contrary, he tells us about the *real* sea which "crawls" under a thin green film made to "fool" people, he compares the "cold" brightness of the sun to a "judgment without indul-gence," he notices the "happy gurgle" of a fountain, a streetcar seat is for him "a dead donkey" drifting, its red plush "thousands of tiny feet," the Self-Taught Man's hand is a "big white worm," etc. Each object would have to be cited, for all are deliberately presented in this fashion. The one most charged with transformations is, of course, the chestnut root, which becomes, succes-sively, "black nail," "boiled leather," "mildew," "dead snake," "vulture's talon," "sealskin," etc., until nausea.

Without trying to limit the book to this particular point of view (though it is an important one), one can say that *existence* in it is character-ized by the presence of interior distances, and that *nausea* is man's unhappy visceral penchant for these distances. The "smile in complicity with things" ends in a grimace: "All the objects that surrounded me were made of the same substance as myself, of a kind of shoddy suffering."

But are we not incited, under these conditions, to accord Roquentin's melancholy celibacy, his lost love, his "wasted life," the lugubrious and laugh-able fate of the Self-Taught Man—all the malediction weighing on the terres-trial world—the status of a superior necessity? Where, then, is freedom? Those who are unwilling to accept this malediction are all the same threat-ened with the supreme moral condemnation: they will be "filthy swine," *salauds*. Everything happens, then, as if Sartre—who can nonetheless hardly be accused of "essentialism"—had, in this book at least, brought the ideas of *nature* and of *tragedy* to their highest point. Once again, to struggle against these ideas is initially to do no more than to confer new powers upon them.

Drowned in the *depth* of things, man ultimately no longer even perceives them: his role is soon limited to experiencing, in their name, totally *humanized* impressions and desires. "In short, it is less a matter of observing the pebble than of installing oneself in its heart and of seeing the world with its eyes . . ."; it is apropos of Francis Ponge that Sartre writes these words. He makes the Roquentin of *Nausea* say: "I *was* the chestnut root." The two positions are not unrelated: it is a matter, in both cases, of thinking "with things" and not *about* them.

Ponge too, as a matter of fact, is not at all concerned to describe. He knows perfectly well, no doubt, that his texts would be of no help to a future archaeologist seeking to discover what a cigarette or candle might have been in our lost civilization. Without our daily frequentation of these objects, Ponge's phrases concerning them are no more than lovely hermetic poems.

On the other hand, we read that the hamper is "annoyed to be in a clumsy position," that the trees in spring "enjoy being fooled" and "release a green vomit," that the butterfly "takes revenge for its long amorphous humiliation as a caterpillar."

Is this really to take the "side" of things, to represent them from "their own point of view"? Ponge obviously cannot be deceiving himself to this degree. The openly psychological and moral anthropomorphism which he continues to practice can have as its goal, on the contrary, only the establishment of a human, general, and absolute order. To assert that he speaks *for* things, *with* them, in their *heart*, comes down, under these conditions, to denying their reality, their opaque presence: in this universe populated by things, they are no longer anything but mirrors for a man that endlessly reflect his own image back to him. Calm, tamed, they stare at man with his own gaze.

Such a *reflection*, in Ponge, is not of course gratuitous. This oscillating movement between man and his natural doubles is that of an active consciousness, concerned to understand itself, to reform itself. Throughout his subtle pages, the smallest pebble, the least stick of wood gives him endless lessons, expresses and judges him at the same time, instructs him in a progress to be made. Thus man's contemplation of the world is a permanent apprenticeship to life, to happiness, to wisdom and to death.

So that ultimately it is a definitive and smiling reconciliation that we are being offered here. Again we have come back to the humanist affirmation: the world is man. But at what cost! For if we abandon the moral perspective of self-improvement, Ponge's *le parti pris des choses* is no longer of any help to us. And if, in particular, we prefer freedom to wisdom, we are obliged to break all these mirrors so artfully arranged by Francis Ponge in order to get back to the hard, dry objects which are behind them, unbroached, as alien as ever.

François Mauriac, who—he said—had once read Ponge's *Hamper* on Jean Paulhan's recommendation, must have remembered very little of this text when he baptized *Hamper Technique* the description of objects advocated in my own writings. Or else I had expressed myself very badly.

To describe things, as a matter of fact, is deliberately to place oneself outside them, confronting them. It is no longer a matter of appropriating them to oneself, of projecting anything onto them. Posited, from the start, as *not being man*, they remain constantly out of reach and are, ultimately, neither comprehended in a natural alliance nor recovered by suffering. To limit oneself to description is obviously to reject all the other modes of approaching the object: sympathy as unrealistic, tragedy as alienating, comprehension as answerable to the realm of science exclusively.

Of course, this last point of view is not negligible. Science is the only honest means man possesses for turning the world around him to account, but it is a material means; however disinterested science may be, it is justified only by the establishment, sooner or later, of utilitarian techniques. Literature has other goals. Only science, on the other hand, can claim to know the *inside* of things. The interiority of the pebble, of the tree, or of the snail which Francis Ponge gives us ridicules science, of course (and even more than Sartre seems to think); hence it in no way represents what is *in* these things, but what man can put into them of his own mind. Having observed certain behavior, with more or less rigor, Ponge is inspired by these appearances to human analogies, and he begins talking about man, always about man, supporting himself on things with a careless hand. It matters little to Ponge that the snail does not "eat" earth, or that the chlorophyllic function is an absorption and not an "exhalation" of carbon gas; his eye is as casual as his recollections of natural history. The only criterion is the truth of the sentiment expressed in terms of these images—of the human sentiment, obviously, and of the human nature which is the nature of all things!

Mineralogy, botany, or zoology, on the contrary, pursue the *knowledge* of textures (internal and external alike), of their organization, of their functioning, and of their genesis. But, outside their domain, these disciplines too are no longer of any use, except for the abstract enrichment of our intelligence. The world around us turns back into a smooth surface, without signification, without soul, without values, on which we no longer have any purchase. Like the workman who has set down the tool he no longer needs, we find ourselves once again *facing* things.

To describe this surface then is merely to constitute this externality and this independence. Probably I have no more to say "about" the box my ink bottle came in than "with" it; if I write that it is a parallellepiped, I make no claim to defining any special essence of it; I have still less intention of handing it over to the reader so that his imagination can seize upon and embellish it with polychrome designs: I should prefer to keep him from doing so, in fact.

The most common criticisms made of such geometric information—"it says nothing to the mind," "a photograph or a diagram would show the shape better," etc.—are strange indeed: wouldn't I have thought of them first of all? As a matter of fact, there is something else involved. The photograph or the diagram aims only at reproducing the object; they are successful to the degree that they suggest as many interpretations (and the same errors) as the model. Formal description, on the other hand, is above all a limitation: when it says "parallelepiped," it knows it achieves no Beyond, but at the same time it cuts short any possibility of seeking one.

To record the distance between the object and myself, and the distances of the object itself (its *exterior* distances, i.e., its measurements), and the distances of objects among themselves, and to insist further on the fact that these are *only distances* (and not divisions), this comes down to establishing that things are here and that they are nothing but things, each limited to itself. The problem is no longer to choose between a happy correspondence and a painful solidarity. There is henceforth a rejection of all complicity.

There is, then, first a rejection of the analogical vocabulary and of traditional humanism, a rejection at the same time of the idea of tragedy, and of any other notion leading to the belief in a profound, and higher, nature of man or of things (and of the two together), a rejection, finally, of every pre-established order.

The sense of sight immediately appears, in this perspective, as the privileged sense, particularly when applied to outlines and contours (rather than to colors, intensities, or transparencies). Optical description is, in effect, the kind which most readily establishes distances: the sense of sight, if it seeks to remain simply that, leaves things in their respective place.

But it also involves risks. Coming to rest, without preparation, on a detail, the sense of sight isolates it, extracts it, seeks to develop it, fails, insists, no longer manages either to develop the detail or return it to its place . . . ; "absurdity" is not far away. Or else contemplation is intensified to the point where everything begins to vacillate, to move, to dissolve . . . ; then "fascination" begins, and "nausea."

Yet these risks remain among the least, and Sartre himself has acknowledged the cleansing power of the sense of sight. Troubled by a contact, by a suspect tactile impression, Roquentin lowers his eyes to his hand: "The pebble was flat, dry on one side, wet and muddy on the other. I was holding it by the edges, my fingers far apart to keep from getting dirty." He no longer understands what has moved him; similarly, a little later on, at the moment of entering his room: "I stopped short, because I felt in my hand a cold object which attracted my attention by a kind of personality. I opened my hand, I looked: I was simply holding the doorknob." Then Roquentin attacks colors, and his eye no longer manages to exercise its displacing action: "The black root did not *get through*, it remained there in my eyes, as a piece that is too big remains stuck in the throat. I could neither accept nor reject it." There has already been the "mauve" of the suspenders and the "suspect transparency" of the glass of beer.

We must work with the means at hand. The sense of sight remains, in spite of everything, our best weapon, especially if it keeps exclusively to outlines. As for its "subjectivity"—principal argument of the opposition—how is its value diminished thereby? Obviously I am concerned, in any case, only with the world as *my point of view* orients it; I shall never know any other. The relative subjectivity of my sense of sight serves me precisely to define *my situation in the world*. I simply keep myself from helping to make this situation a servitude.

Thus, though Roquentin thinks "the sense of sight is an abstract invention, a scoured, simplified idea, a human idea," it nonetheless remains, between the world and myself, the most effective operation.

For effectiveness is the point. To measure the distances—without futile regret, without hatred, without despair—between what is separated, will permit us to identify what is *not* separated, what *is one*, since it is false that everything is double—false, or at least provisional. Provisional with regard to man, that is our hope. False already with regard to things: once scoured clean, they no longer refer to anything except to themselves, without a flaw for us to slip into, without a tremor.

One question persists: Is it possible to escape tragedy?

Today its rule extends to all my feelings and all my thoughts; it conditions me utterly. My body can be satisfied, my heart content, my consciousness remains unhappy. I assert that this unhappiness *is situated* in space and time, like every unhappiness, like everything in this world. I assert that man, someday, will free himself from it. But of this future I possess no proof. For me, too, it is a wager. "Man is a sick animal," Unamuno wrote in *The Tragic Sense of Life*; the wager consists in believing he can be cured, and that it would therefore be a mistake to imprison him in his disease. I have nothing to lose. This wager, in any event, is the only reasonable one.

I have said that I possessed no proof. It is easy to perceive, nonetheless, that the systematic *tragedification* of the universe I live in is often the result of a deliberate intention. This suffices to cast a doubt on any proposition tending to posit tragedy as natural and definitive. Now, from the moment doubt has appeared, I cannot do otherwise than seek still farther.

This struggle, I shall be told, is precisely the tragic illusion par excellence: if I seek to combat the idea of tragedy, I have already succumbed to it; and it is so natural to take objects as a refuge . . . perhaps. But perhaps not. And, in that case. . . .

GERMAINE BRÉE

Heroes of Our Time: The Stranger

"En tout cas, comment se limiter à
l'idée que rien n'a de sens et qu'il faille
désespérer de tout?"

Meursault, the hero of *L'Etranger*, is a kind of Adam, a man content just
to live and who asks no questions. But like Melville's Billy Budd, Meursault
kills a man. He is then judged to be guilty, but why? The prosecutor, lawyer,
and chaplain answer the question in conventional semi-social, semi-religious,
Occidental terms, but these officials represent abstract entities and their
answers mean nothing to Meursault nor to a simple-minded man like Meursault's friend, Céleste; quite obviously their explanations do not apply to the
case as Camus devised it.

But as the tale develops it seems clear that Meursault's error lies
precisely in his estrangement. He acts in a human situation as though human
relationships, and therefore responsibilities, do not exist, and before he
knows it he is involved in Raymond's elementary but violent drama. That
Meursault killed the Arab is a fact. That his act was not premeditated and
that there was provocation is also a fact. But at the trial what both prosecu-

From *Camus.* © 1959 The State University of Rutgers.

tion and defense present to the jury are all the unrelated events in Meursault's life between his mother's death and the murder; these events are presented in a logically organized whole as the basis of an interpretation of Meursault's personality. As Meursault sits in bewildered surprise through this reconstruction of his crime, he begins to feel that he is being condemned to death because he was found guilty of not crying at his mother's funeral. And in a sense he is right. In fact he is condemned, according to Camus himself, "because he does not play the game." He is a stranger to society, because he refuses to make any concession whatsoever to its codes and rituals. He sees no relation at all between his mother's death and the fact that he goes to see a comic film two days later, and he establishes none. And, seeing through his eyes, we are almost in complete agreement with him. He is, as Camus himself has said, the man who refuses to lie.

Meursault's attitude at first merely reveals how arbitrary and superficial are the codes with which we cover up the stark incomprehensibility of life; for example, we can feel it is enough, in the presence of death, if we simply refrain from smoking a cigarette. With a certain fierce humor Camus uses his hero to shake us out of our complacency and to ridicule our smugness. But when Meursault goes even further, refusing to humor the prosecutor's Christian pathos because he sees no relation between his own act and the crucifix, refusing to take the "leads" of his lawyer, which play on a stock set of conventional emotional values, he becomes a kind of social martyr, a man who "dies rather than lie" in answer to a question. It is not, however, the satire of a society and the miscarriage of justice that give the tale its fundamental significance. With the shooting of the Arab, Meursault tells us, "everything began," and more specifically still, "everything began" in the prison after Marie's one and only visit, "everything," that is Meursault's inner transformation.

Once or twice in the course of the tale we catch a glimpse of an earlier Meursault, for example the student who had once been to Paris: presumably he had not always lived in the passive, autonomous state in which we find him. In this respect his precursor, Patrice (*La Mort heureuse*), gives us an excellent clue to Meursault's adventure which, like his own, is essentially spiritual in nature. At one stage in his spiritual career Patrice had aspired to become similar to an object, to live timelessly and to be one with the world. Meursault seems to have achieved this state at the beginning of *L'Etranger*. "Meursault, for me," writes Camus, is "a poor and naked man, in love with the sun which leaves no shadows. He is far from being totally deprived of sensitivity for he is animated by a passion, profound because it is tacit, the passion for the absolute and for truth. It is still a negative truth, the truth of being and feeling, but a truth without which no conquest of the self or the world is possible." That is why, until the very end, Meursault is the man who answers but never asks a question, and all his answers alarm a society which cannot bear to look at the truth.

But the revolver shot jolts Meursault out of his purely negative state. At the time he is aware that he has committed an irreparable act: "I understood that I had destroyed the equilibrium of the day, the unusual silence of a beach where I had been happy." As in the case of Dimitri Karamazov, the real crime is not the one for which Meursault is being tried, but another which he will understand fully at the end when he accedes to a new level of awareness, conquering the world and himself as he grasps the nature of that happiness of which he had had a vague premonition on the beach.

Immediately after his imprisonment, Meursault—like Patrice in Prague after the murder of Zagreus—plunges into a new timeless world, the endless, uniform prison day. There he discovers three inexhaustible but completely closed subjective worlds: the world of memory; the world of sleep; and, as he scans over and over again a newspaper item (a murder story), the world of human solitude. Thus he "kills time," living, as it were, a timeless existence, but an existence which brings him only apathetic sadness. To him in his prison, his face is now that of a stranger, an exile.

The final revelation comes like a flash just before Meursault's death. In spite of Meursault, the prison chaplain has come to speak of forgiveness, of an after-life in which all may be redeemed. For the first time since he shot the Arab Meursault is jolted out of his apathy and in an access of rage he violently shakes the priest. There is no after-life. There is only one life, his life as he knew it—the swims and the beaches, the evenings and Marie's light dresses and soft body—an intense, glorious life that needs no redeeming, no regrets, no tears. Why cry at his mother's funeral? Why lament his own death? After all he is no different from any other human being: all are condemned to death just as he is, except that he knows both the glory of life and the unjustifiable nature of death. His crime and his revelation are as one. He destroyed and is destroyed. For this destruction there is no explanation, excuse, or compensation. The anguished hours of self-torture in his prison cell are over; he no longer calculates endlessly how he may escape. Defiant and lucid, he will go to his death happy: "As if my great outburst of anger had purged me of evil, emptied now of all hope, face to face with a night heavy with signs and stars, I abandoned myself to the tender indifference of the world. Feeling it . . . so fraternal at last, I knew I had been happy, and that I was still happy. So that all might be consummated, so that I might feel less alone, all that was left for me to wish was that there should be many spectators the day of my execution and that they should greet me with cries of hatred."

Meursault here becomes a sacrificial victim, his end is an apotheosis, the equivalent of Patrice's "happy death," a descent into the sea and sun, a re-integration into the cosmos. The stranger has in his prison cell, on the brink of death, found his kingdom: the irreplaceable, every-moment life of an ordinary human being who by an inexplicable decree of fate is destined to death. Meursault, as Camus conceived him, must disappear with this revelation.

It is clear that Meursault's initial mental attitude proves inadequate to cope with even the simplest of lives. The very essence of *l'absurde* in his case is that out of indifference he linked forces with violence and death, not with love and life. Like Parsifal in the legend of the Fisher-King he fails to ask any question and thereby gravely errs. In *L'Etranger* Camus thus suggests that in the face of the absurd no man can afford passively just to exist. To fail to question the meaning of the spectacle of life is to condemn both ourselves, as individuals, and the whole world to nothingness.

ROGER SHATTUCK

Two Inside Narratives:
Billy Budd *and* L'Etranger

Like two mineral specimens different in color and texture yet remarkably similar in structure, Melville's last novel and Camus's first seem designed for comparison. A few scholars have remarked the kinship without analyzing it at length. Direct influence can be ruled out, since Camus read *Billy Budd* after having written *L'Etranger*. Thus we are left very much in the clear with something suggestive to assay. The evident value of comparing the independent approach of two major authors to a similar theme is here augmented by the fact that the significance of both works remains in dispute.

The two narratives turn on the same, essentially equivocal situation. From one point of view, a real crime, not of passion or premeditation, but of impulse, is described as an innocent action. From an opposing point of view, a spiritually innocent man discovers and ultimately affirms his guilt. "Innocence and guilt . . . in effect changed places," writes Melville just before Billy's trial. In both books this ambivalent situation arises through the rigid application of a system of justice to a murder that follows a series of fortuitous misdemeanors. Billy, for example, spills soup in Claggart's path. Two days after his mother's funeral Meursault goes to a Fernandel movie with his new girlfriend. In each case a lengthy trial scene leading to the death sentence reveals the narrowness and distortion of the "justice" defined respectively by the British Articles of War in 1797 and by the Napoleonic

From *Texas Studies in Literature and Language* 4, no. 3 (Autumn 1962). © 1962 by the University of Texas Press.

Criminal Code. Yet neither man defends himself against the charges, nor does he show any remorse. Thus the two crimes remain inwardly unjudged and produce no moral anguish, even though both Billy and Meursault accept their guilt. In his final moment Billy cries out, "God bless Captain Vere!" and dies peacefully. Meursault finds the prosecutor's case against him "plausible" and faces the facts in the middle of his trial: "J'ai senti alors quelque chose qui soulevait toute la salle et, pour la première fois, j'ai compris que j'étais coupable." The statement turns on the fact that at this point Meursault still cannot disengage what he inwardly knows himself to be from what society judges him to be.

This cross-play of innocence and guilt leads directly into the characters of the two heroes. Though given very different backgrounds and temperaments, they immediately reveal that something has already dislocated their entire mode of existence, and has produced their unlikely but alluring innocence. Of Billy, Melville states that in moments of strong feeling he was "apt to develop an organic hesitancy, in fact more or less of a stutter or even worse." This single flaw suffices to signify a mysterious imbalance in his character. And here we strike upon the first real illumination afforded by the comparison of these two novels. Meursault's inability to reply to any question that demands a choice or a preference, his habitual response of "Cela m'est égal," amounts to a metaphysical stutter more serious than Billy's. Their inarticulateness, the impediment between their consciousness and the world, is not accidental but essential. It defines Billy and Meursault as truncated men whose actions must necessarily appear ambivalent.

Under longer scrutiny these similarities of theme yield to extensive differences in the narrative style employed. Billy's story comes to us through the eyes and mind of a shadowy narrator who speaks alternately as a keen witness (who nevertheless misses many of the crucial scenes), and as a singularly obtuse and tendentious commentator on the events. His refracting presence has been neglected by all but one critic, Lawrance Thompson, who makes it the basis for interpreting the story as essentially ironic, a masked quarrel with God. From behind this further ambiguity of style, however, one fact emerges clearly: none of the principal characters changes in the course of the action, Billy least of all. "The handsome sailor," as Melville repeatedly calls him, is born to his status of "natural" election, learns nothing from experience, and maintains to the end his upright character and resignation to misfortune. We learn that, though a foundling, he is "evidently no ignoble one." Though many critics have proposed a major shift in Billy's attitude toward life and death during the off-stage interview in which Captain Vere tells him the sentence, nothing in the text supports this hypothesis. Even with allowances for irony, Billy remains the "noble barbarian," a second

Adam with no taint of the serpent but a stutter, an angel of God. Accordingly, his punishment is imposed solely on the basis of his deed, without consideration for his innocence of character and lack of evil intent.

The exact opposite hold for Meursault. The trial focuses not on his deed but on the purported insensitivity and moral depravity of every part of his life. And, unlike Billy, he changes. The unpremeditated and fateful shooting, plus the ritualized trial, conspire to capsize Meursault's inner equilibrium.

The change in his state of being can be detected in the narrative style which, totally unlike that of *Billy Budd*, appears at first to be restricted to the hero's immediate sensations recorded without the categories of civilized living. From the outset, however, one stumbles over sentences which protrude above the flatness of the prose. Very early in the story, for instance, during the scene of the wake, Meursault breaks through the surface of his monotone: "J'ai eu un moment l'impression ridicule qu'ils étaient là pour me juger." One barely notices the shift in point of view. Some sixty pages later, after the much discussed explosion of metaphors in the passage on the shooting on the beach, Meursault finds himself oddly afraid of the examining magistrate and makes this highly sophisticated observation about his fear: "Je reconnaissais en même temps que c'était ridicule parce que, somme toute, c'était moi le criminel." This is no transparent sensibility. He is beginning to catch sight of himself. The primitive first person singular of passive sensation has gradually secreted beside itself another, highly penetrating person of reflection. And this bifurcation of sensibility asserts itself in the style in the shape of a double *je*, which functions simultaneously as first person and as third person looking back astonished. It is the reverse of Diderot's or Stendhal's mimetic and enthusiastic *il*, which they frequently brandish as if it were a first person. In *L'Etranger* Camus displays a consciousness discovering itself in a crucial process, recollection of which is usually irretrievable from the hinterland of childhood.

This emergence of self, first seen stirring in the syntax, is brought out further by an equally subtle device which raises the events of the story out of the dead level of meaninglessness. There is an innocent-looking passage at the end of the second chapter that seems to close us out of Meursault's life by closing the whole dreary incident of his mother's death and burial. But not so:

> J'ai fermé mes fenêtres et en revenant j'ai vu dans la glace un bout de table où ma lampe à alcool voisinait avec des morceaux de pain. J'ai pensé que c'était toujours un dimanche de tiré, que maman était maintenant enterrée, que j'allais reprendre mon travail et que, somme toute, il n'y avait rien de changé.

This instant, in which Meursault glimpses just a corner of his existence in the mirror, this little still-life image of his surroundings, is the first of a series of happenings that force Meursault to see himself, to reflect on his life. And we are carried back into the story instead of being sealed out of it. The instances of Meursault's self-beholding become increasingly explicit: the bizarre "automatic" woman in the restaurant, the newspaper clipping in his cell, the "sad, severe" face he sees reflected in his mess bowl, the startling sound of his own voice when he finds he is talking to himself, the journalist staring fixedly at him in the courtroom, and the testimony of the witnesses talking on and on about him. Finally Meursault's lawyer reviews all the events of the case, using the first person, a convention that turns Meursault into a fascinated and helpless spectator of his own life: "Moi j'ai pensé que c'était m'écarter encore de l'affaire, me réduire à zéro et, en un certain sens, se substituer à moi." This series of disturbing self-confrontations leaves Meursault divided and weakened at a time when he wants for the first time to be *comme tout le monde*, a normal human being. He never has his wish. The chaplain's visit and offer of absolution and intercession provoke from Meursault violent self-affirmation as a criminal outcast. Thus at the end he strives to reassemble his divided sensibility. He strikes out not so much at the "absurdity" of his life, as we are frequently told, as at a threat to the one role left to him: that of embittered but courageous victim who wants people's hate and not their help.

The contrast in action is, therefore, pronounced. Billy's fate is virtually given in his birth with its obscure defect. Self-sacrifice leaves him unchanged. Meursault, still an uncomprehending sleepwalker in the murder scene on the beach, finally calls fate down on his head when he grasps the meaning of his act. Self-sacrifice makes him a man.

At this point a change of method is required to search beyond the set of similarities and differences examined up to now. The science of crystallography discovered over a century ago insists that in comparing mineral specimens one must not be content with looking at them but must go on to examine a beam of light that has passed through them. The discovery of plane-polarized light led to major revelations about the internal molecular structure of crystals. The final stage of the comparative method applied to related works like *Billy Budd* and *L'Etranger* may be to regard them in series, seeking the clearest meaning they transmit together.

It is here that Melville's cryptic and cautionary subtitle, *an Inside Narrative*, takes on significance for both novels. Applied in the present context to Camus's novel, it appropriately calls attention to the deepest movement of the book's action: a human consciousness undergoing mitosis, an inner division experienced very late by a physically mature man. We witness the process from inside through the ambiguous and shifting use of a double *je*. Meursault's final self-affirmation as a condemned man is a truly heroic effort to bring the parts back together in defiance of society's judgment and of Christian forgiveness.

Meursault's separation from himself and return, sighted through Melville's complementary action, allows fresh insight into the character structure of *Billy Budd*. Billy never comes unstuck from himself because he already belongs to a larger division. In Melville's story we are symbolically carried inside the microcosm of one individual broken into three parts: Captain Vere standing for the pride of both reason and authority, Claggart, who represents "depravity according to nature," and Billy, who embodies ingenuous goodness. None of the three is pure, and none is a whole man. *The Indomitable* puts to sea less as the ship of state or society than as the ship of a complex individual. Under the stress of social and political upheaval lengthily described in the opening chapters, this living unit, this multiple man sacrifices one part of himself in order to maintain discipline. The whole pulse of the novel implies that such a sacrifice must be lethal. *Billy Budd* is anything but a "testament of acceptance," as it has often been described since E. L. G. Watson's article in 1933. Nor is it (as it has been labelled by an eloquent lecturer for a society working to abolish the institution) the only novel ever written in defense of capital punishment. In unmistakable allegory Melville presents the possibility of man's inward division and the accompanying dangers of self-destruction.

Held up together to the light, these two novels have an iridescent quality, a flickering of implied meanings ranging from Christian atonement, to the embodiment of fate in social situations, to the sinfulness of God himself. Despite flaws of artificial style and some labored symbolism in both books, they are true gems with the capacity to refract light in multiple ways. But the clearest beam they transmit when set in the proper alignment emanates from a single area of experience. These two inside narratives reveal man's consciousness deadlocked with its own most awe-inspiring work—civilization—here in the form of "justice" under law. The particular natures of Billy and Meursault lead to exceptional treatments of this theme, faced less squarely and less often in fiction than we should like to believe.

We have come to think of the novel as the exhibiting of a hero constantly testing, risking, and extending himself in some form of play-acting inspired by the realization of being alive: Robinson Crusoe to Rastignac to Proust's Marcel. Stendhal's most characteristic creations prove themselves in moments of intense crisis by their ability to improvise both action and emotion. In novels so markedly different as those of D. H. Lawrence and Virginia Woolf, the heroes, after first ascertaining the strictures of life around them, begin to recast their inner being in response to glimpsed possibilities of experience. But the two heroes we have been examining refuse to engage in this energetic psychological prospecting in the face of the "forms" of civilized existence. Billy never deviates from his given character and has no qualms about himself. True, he fears a flogging and is stunned by his impulsive violence; but he sleeps soundly the night before his execution. Meursault, just a few degrees more sophisticated than Billy, begins in a comparable state of mind, is then wrenched far enough out of this restricted sensibility to see himself as others see him, goes on to refuse that knowledge in the scene with the chaplain, and at the end reasserts his original "simple" consciousness of himself as a man. Thus they both stubbornly remain on a level with the *mécanique* of justice that condemn them and do not evade it by any subtle psychological contortion.

In an era of post-Freudian plastic surgery of the soul, it is this flatfootedness of character that gives the two books their archaic tone and haunting appeal. Billy's final blessing and Meursault's final curse grow out of the same primitive moral awareness of how man has constructed around himself the potential instrument of his own destruction. Melville and Camus do not squander their distress on the future of civilization. They know that in the struggle to live with it and ahead of it, it is the self that suffers and the self that may perish. Save him.

ROBERT CHAMPIGNY

Ethics and Aesthetics in The Stranger

What is meant by "ethics" is to be explained in a preliminary analysis. What is meant by "aesthetics" will be elucidated in the course of the development.

Ethical values are concerned basically with activities, not things, not motions. Activities can be classified. We may isolate a class of "ethical" activities, that is to say, of activities on which judgments of the ethical type can bear with relevance. Thus we may decide to call "ethical" (ethically good, or bad, or both), the class of activities which are effectively designed to remove or produce pain, or both. We may also isolate an ethical aspect or element in activities which, globally, would not be classified under the heading of ethics. Thus it is customary to speak of the ethics of a game. The designation "ethics of activities" can be used to cover both cases.

Instead of being content to consider particular activities as members of classes of activities, we may also try to see them as constituent parts of a whole. The totality in question is not that of an object (a work of art, a machine); it is the totality of one existence, one life that is probably, though not necessarily, human: it depends on how far we are willing to extend the notion of activity. In this case, a positive ethical value is granted to a particular activity insofar as it contributes to the composition of a coherent existential whole. Such a totality I call an ethical or existential figure.

From *Camus: A Collection of Critical Essays.* © 1962 Prentice-Hall Inc.

According to this type of valuation, "ethical validity" and "existential coherence" are synonymous. The ethics of existence which is thus defined differs from the ethics of activities: a set of activities, each of which is ethically right in its class, may be devoid of existential coherence and fail to compose an ethical figure. Existential coherence must be distinguished from formal coherence. Temporality is involved, which requires a dialectical approach. The word "ethics" in the title refers primarily to the ethics of existence.

"Value" and "meaning" are partially synonymous. Something is given a value, or meaning, when it is comprehended. Comprehension may be formal, cognitive, aesthetic, ethical, philosophical. In a scheme of comprehension, the material to be comprehended is made intelligible with the help of tools of comprehension: relations, patterns, frames. These tools themselves are comprehended in action. Taken by themselves, they are not intelligible: a notion cannot make itself intelligible. Consider these questions: "What is there beyond space? When did time begin?" Such tools, in the scheme they help build, are basic, absolute. Taken by themselves, they are absurd. "Absolute" and "absurd" are partially synonymous.

The Platonic arsenal of ideas and the god of the theologians were invented to serve as tools of comprehension. Taken by themselves, they are absurd. I can make something intelligible by using a pattern of finality or the relation of causality. Taken by themselves, causality and finality are unintelligible. I can try to make finality cognitively intelligible by dissolving it in a causal network: this is the task of a physicalistic psychology. I can try to give a meaning to causality by fitting it into a pattern of finality; every informed activity accomplishes this implicitly. This paragraph should make clear the pointlessness of the traditional bouts between freedom and determinism. It also suggests what is philosophically wrong with certain psychological concepts: thus "motivation" is a mixture of "cause" and "intention" which discloses a confusion between finality and interiority on the one hand, causality and exteriority on the other.

In a perspective of interiority, this-life is an autonomous whole, an absolute. From the outside, this absolute appears unconnected, hence absurd. The concept of this-life is a totality concept in a scheme of comprehension. It is supposed to help give meaning, not to be given meaning. If you prefer, it has meaning insofar as it gives meaning. If I want to give an existential value, or meaning, to something, I have to see it as part of this-life and make it assume a constitutive function through the use of a pattern of comprehension which may be finality, which may also be destiny (but not causality). Destiny is the pattern which fits the figure of Meursault. What is meant by "destiny" will be explained.

Let us now suppose that a certain life appears too lacking in coherence for me to consider it as an autonomous whole. I may be content to salvage certain activities, I shall proceed according to the ethics of activities. I may also consider this life in a perspective of exteriority, as one life-unit, as a member of the class of lives, or human lives. In this case, the value, or meaning, is cognitive, not ethical. I provide an explanation, not a justification.

In order to bestow an ethical value on a life which is lacking in inner value, I have to see it as part of a whole. I can do so through a confusion of conceptual modalities: I confuse generality and totality; I mistake a class concept for a totality concept. This is made easier by the fact that names of class concepts are generally written in the singular. "Man, oh, not men," exclaimed Shelley, thus providing political totalitarianism with a motto. The phrase "desire to belong" reveals this attempt and this confusion, since the verb "to belong" may mean either "to be a member of a class" or "to be part of a whole." The image of a model individual may be involved in the process, so that the conceptual confusion extends to the mode of individuality—consider the ideas of communion and of the mystical body.

I call pseudo-ethics the theoretical or practical attempt to give meaning, value, to a life by viewing it as part of a whole. The totality in question is a pseudo-totality. The prefix "pseudo" indicates a contradiction between the end (understanding, valuation) and the means (confusion, hypnotism) Pseudo-ethics is distinct both from the ethics of activities and from the ethics of existence.

A team-activity may be considered as composing an objective totality; but it does not exhaust an existence. The actor plays a role; but he remains distinct from it. The pseudo-ethical goal is to transmute an existence into an essence (character, role) comprehended (saved) in a socio-religious pseudo-world. This attempt does not prevent the organism from continuing to live and die its own life and death: the transfiguration is a mask. But this is all that may be needed to set the mind at rest. Theoretically incorrect, the attempt may be reasonably successful in practice, as long as the mask is not disturbed. Meursault may appear to some as a disturbing factor.

In the second part of *The Stranger*, the ethos of Meursault is confronted with pseudo-ethics. From a philosophical standpoint, that is what the trial consists in. The following passage reports the word of the *juge d'instruction* (examining magistrate):

"He told me that it was impossible, that everybody believed in God, even those who turned away from his face. This was his conviction and if he should come to doubt it, his life would no longer have a meaning."

The question appears to be: "Is the class of believers-in-God identical with the class of human beings or a sub-class thereof?" To understand how the answer to this question can affect the meaning of the life of the magistrate, I have to assume that the said magistrate confuses generality and totality. Mankind is implicitly conceived as a whole constituted through communion. The life of the magistrate is supposed to be given a meaning, a value, through this magic participation. But Meursault is a man and he does not commune: "How can one be a Persian?" asked the Parisians of Montesquieu. If Meursault is taken seriously, the concept of mankind as a value-giving whole is shattered.

The jury decides that Meursault cannot be salvaged. He is a monster: on the one hand, he is a member of the human race (animals are not invited to courtroom festivals); on the other hand, he does not belong to the society-of-men (mystical body). His death will efface this discrepancy between generality and totality. Then the priest tries to salvage Meursault for the divine city.

The global effect of Meursault's retort to the priest is a rejection of pseudo-values and the affirmation of existential values. But the impassioned words of Meursault bear little resemblance to the elegant discourse of Socrates in the *Apology*. The affirmation of existential values is mostly implicit. As in the rest of the book, they are shown rather than told: the explicit rejection of pseudo-values is an implicit affirmation of values. Still, it is apparent that two kinds of valuation are involved. On the one hand, Meursault seems bent on leveling everything. On the other, he suggests differences in value: "I had been right, I was still right." Why does not Meursault say instead: "What difference does it make to be right or wrong?"

In a pseudo-ethical process, uniqueness is dissolved in a generality, then generality is misinterpreted as totality. Meursault's speech takes us explicitly one step back, implicitly two. He adopts the perspective of exteriority. He considers his life as one life-unit among others. In this way, instead of retiring within the subjective absolute, he can speak to the priest. But he refuses to smuggle a part-whole relation, a false interiority, under the individual-general relation. Thus pseudo-values are expelled. Each life is a member of the class of lives. All lives are mortal. All lives are equal before death: "Only one fate was to elect me and with me billions of privileged beings who, like him [the priest], said they were my brothers." It is under the cloak of such words as "brother" that the leap from generality to totality is often effected.

But if Meursault explicitly considers his life from the outside as a life-unit, he has to be alive to do so. He has to live a unique life in order to be able to speak about life in general. In this perspective of interiority there may be values, namely, whatever helps constitute the whole as a whole. The rightness which Meursault claims is apparently one of these values.

In a previous essay, I set out to analyze the ethos of Meursault. Concerning the relation between ethics and pseudo-ethics, I tried to show how the trial brought the logic of the character into relief. Concerning the relation between ethics and aesthetics, I noted: "The book holds together because the character holds together and vice-versa." I am going to analyze what this formula indicates and conceals.

The aesthetic mode of apprehension has often been called a kind of "knowledge"; it has been said that aesthetical expression could establish a kind of "truth." It might be more judicious to dump these two harpies in the lap of the philosopher of science, who clamors for them. On the other hand, it would be a good opening move to consider the aesthetic mode of apprehension and expression as a mode of comprehension. Aesthetic values (aesthetic meaning) have the same theoretical extension as cognitive values: they can be tried on any object. But the aesthetic mode of intelligibility is based on the part-whole relation; it uses a perspective of interiority. The cognitive mode of intelligibility, on the other hand, is based on the individual-general relation; it uses a perspective of exteriority. The aesthetic mode of comprehension has a basic similarity with the ethical (existential) mode. But aesthetic values bear on objects, ethical values on activities and existence.

In *The Stranger*, the relation between ethics and aesthetics can be studied on two levels: the aesthetic aspect and the ethical aspect will first be considered as elements of the fictional field; then they will be considered as informing, each in its own way, the whole fictional world.

The ethical element is provided by Meursault's account of his behavior and by his meditations; the aesthetic element is provided by his descriptions of the physical *ambiance*. The first chapters of the book, on the whole, depict a peaceful accord between Meursault's ethos and the physical conditions. A basic move in the aesthetic process is to turn thing into quality (poetry), or at least to subordinate thing to quality (novel). The descriptions in *The Stranger* emphasize pervasive qualities rather than limited things—air and light, sea and sky. Quick notations suffice to make the reader's imagination enjoy what is fluid, expansive, non-finite, sensuous. But there are intimations that the accord between the physical and ethical is threatened: the light and the heat tend at times to be overwhelming. Thus the episode of the murder on the beach is prepared.

As far as the ethical element is concerned, the episode is a blank: there was no action, but an event, an accident. On the other hand, the aesthetic suggestions scattered so far in the narration converge and coalesce. The episode which is most unintelligible ethically is also the episode which is most intelligible aesthetically.

The physical elements which were emphasized are now fused together, mainly through metaphors: the "breath" of the heat is also that of the sea; light falls like a "rain." An aesthetic whole is obtained through the interpenetration of qualities. The events are taken out of their temporal context so as to become part of this whole: "It was two hours since the day had ceased to move, two hours since it had cast anchor in this ocean of boiling metal." A metaphysical experience is suggested. Meursault is drawn into a domain which ethical values cannot penetrate, at least at the moment, but which is open to aesthetic values. This is marked by the abrupt rise of the metaphors.

Essentially, what the description attempts to evoke is power. Even as a scientific notion, power remains metaphysical: energy is the metaphysical concept kept by physics. Some of the metaphors tend to make the direction of the power appear as a purpose; they are the first steps in the composition of a god. The god whom the description does not quite bring out is Apollo Loxias, the sun-god and source of oracles who "fated" Orestes. Trying to account for his action, or rather for his motions, Meursault will say that it was "because of the sun." He does not try to justify himself, but to explain. In the context of the book, this explanation points to an aesthetic reason rather than to a scientific cause. In the murder episode, Meursault is a resistance and a conductor.

At the end of the book, we are presented again with a detached aesthetic tableau: that of the starry night. This time the aesthetic element does not eliminate the ethical element. The ethos of Meursault has won its fight against pseudo-ethics. As in the beginning, but in a tragic key, there is a harmony between the ethical and the aesthetic elements. The "fraternity" which Meursault says that he feels with the "universe" contrasts with the brotherhood which he has refused: communion in a socio-religious pseudo-world. An analogy can be drawn between the spectacle of the night and the speech of Meursault as I have analyzed it.

Let us consider each star as analogous to one life. We do not apprehend the spectacle in the manner of Pascal, trying to pass on his terror to an imaginary reader. We do not apprehend it in the manner of Valéry, or Pythagoras, who imagined a music of the spheres, that is to say, mathematical proportions. We consider the stars as members of a class, similar and unconnected. Each star, or life, taken by itself, is an absolute. This does not mean that there is no unity in the spectacle. But the unity is not the image of a human or divine city. It is purely aesthetic: the cosmic quality of the night is what unifies.

This final accord has been prepared. The aesthetic element almost disappears during the account of the trial. The human pseudo-world has closed upon Meursault and he has to reject it as he is rejected. Yet, half-way through this second part of the book, the aesthetic element is glimpsed. There is an evocation of the evening air and sky which serves as a transition between the afternoon on the beach and the vision of the starry night.

Let us, for a moment, allow images to unfold their fluid logic. Meursault kills the man who stands between him and the spring. The sun directs Meursault toward the spring. The day hastens toward night. Meursault goes to his death. The sun is the power of life. The work of life is death. Meursault kills because of the sun. The spring, death, and night are superimposed. Meursault has to pierce through the human pseudo-world in order to reach the spring. The human obstacle into which he fires and this pseudo-world are superimposed. Thus there are signals between the ethical and the aesthetic elements as between two ships which are to meet.

If we now consider the book in its unity, the ethical and aesthetic elements become part of a composition which may itself be considered either as an aesthetic or as an ethical whole. The way in which I have presented the play between the two elements suggests an aesthetic composition.

Beauty is harmony. This definition may appear less otiose if it is noted that harmony implies tension. What is to be avoided is flatness on the one hand, disparateness on the other. Harmony is a play of opposition and fusion. We are dealing with a narration. The pattern of harmony can be unfolded temporally. The global arrangement of the two elements can be represented as follows. A circle and its horizontal diameter are drawn. This diameter is oriented so as to represent the direction of time. The upper half of the circumference represents the aesthetic element, the lower half the ethical. There is a meeting of the two elements at both ends of the temporal line. It is notable that though the narration covers a much greater span of time, the passages which emphasize the aesthetic element are ordered in a one-day sequence: the funeral in the morning, the murder at the beginning of the afternoon, the glimpse of the evening, the starry night. The upper half of the circumference thus represents the solar revolution. The zenith of the aesthetic element (of cosmic power) corresponds to the nadir of the ethical element (its disappearance).

If the book as a whole is to be considered as composing an ethical figure, it will be viewed as a monologue, not as a novel. The descriptions (the aesthetic element) will be interpreted as expressions of the ethos of Meursault. Actually, it is as a monologue that the book is ostensibly presented. The story is told in the first person and this first person is not limited to the introduction of events: the narrator is also a commentator. He affirms his presence outside and above the human character caught in the flow of events. This is most obvious when a present tense is used: "Now I think that it was a false impression. . . . I still do not know why. . . . I can say that. . . . I think I slept. . . . " More globally, the use of the compound tense ("j'ai vu"; "il m'a dit") instead of the historic tense contributes to the distinction between the narrator and the character: the auxiliary, in the present tense, goes with the narrator; the past participle goes with the character.

Some commentators have expressed doubt as to the likelihood of certain passages: the metaphor-laden description of the murder episode, the speech to the priest. If we insist on likelihood, there is something more basically disturbing: when and to whom does Meursault tell the story that we have been reading? However, this is reasoning as if the subject matter preceded its treatment, whereas the contrary is true: the book creates its subject matter. We are thrown back on questions of likelihood only when the work is lacking in internal coherence, when we feel the need to account for the scattered pieces and we try the exterior criterion which is valid in the judgment of historical studies. In other words, art is artificial and great art is greatly artificial. The list might begin with *The Iliad*—which does not mean that what is greatly artificial is great art. What is to the point is whether the book is coherent aesthetically and whether it composes a coherent existential figure. If it does, I am no more interested in the likelihood of *The Stranger* than in the likelihood of the Gospel. The consideration of ethical values involves no epistemological restrictions. The subject, whether it be Meursault, Joan of Arc, a friend, or myself, has to be imagined. No doubt, I do not have to imagine my own life in order to experience it; but as subject matter, it has to be imagined.

Actually, the situation is even more strange than I have suggested. The "now" of the narrator is mutable. On the first page I read: "I shall take the bus"; and in the next paragraph, without a transition: "I took the bus." Further on I read: "Today is Saturday"; yet the story of this Saturday is told in the past. The same shift in tenses occurs in the last chapter. My task is to show how the status of the narrator helps compose an existential figure.

I see two patterns of intelligibility which can befit such a composition. One is finality: this is the pattern recommended by Sartre. The other is destiny: this is the pattern which fits *The Stranger*. By destiny, I do not mean causality; I do not mean the general fate to which Meursault alludes; I do not mean the evil genius who seems personally attached to some character and who performs like a judo champion; i.e., whatever the character does boomerangs against him. All this takes place in a perspective of exteriority. The cause is exterior to the effect; fate is exterior to the one who is fated.

Understood in this way, fate can be used in an aesthetic, not in an ethical, whole.

Destiny, in the sense here used, has to shape the ethical figure from the inside. What has happened must be internalized, so that the life in question no longer appears as fashioned by the events, but as identical with them; the haphazard series of events is transfigured into an existential whole. This operation I call an existential totalization, as distinct from an existential project (pattern of finality). It is as a narrator, not as a character moving with the events, that Meursault can effect this totalization. Finality and causality can appear before the fact; I plan and I make use of causality in my plans. Destiny can only appear after the fact. The compound past tense catches some of the flavor of the Greek perfect.

The study of the character can reveal a static and somewhat abstract ethos. We look for recurrences of the same type of behavior; they indicate certain virtues and we try to see whether these virtues help compose a coherent static figure. What is missing is the unique process, the existential dialectics, the temporal dynamics which the word "destiny" is here intended to imply.

As a narrator placed at the end of the series, Meursault can capture events which the ethical element did not penetrate: the courtroom comedy as well as the episode on the beach. But this recuperation is only a collection. A decisive move in the ethical transfiguration is the speech to the priest. It expresses mainly the negative side of the operation. Meursault as it were sterilizes, neutralizes, the sum of events. According to his own words, he purges himself of "evil," that is to say, of the temptation of pseudo-values. He refuses to repent, to deny what has happened, to be robbed of his material. On the other hand, however, it is interesting to note that he rejects the possibility of a pattern of finality: "What mattered to me . . . the lives that one chooses, the fates that one elects, since only one fate was to elect me . . . ?" The irony on "choice," a holy word for Sartre, shows that Meursault is not afflicted, or blessed, with sartritis. He does not say, "My life is such as I chose it"; he says, or implies, "My life is such as I see it and have always seen it."

The rightness which he claims is important to him. His philosophy will be "justified" on the morning of the execution. The wisdom of Meursault is the first unifying factor which contributes to the composition of an existential whole. The events now seem to have been accumulated by fate, or chance, in order to prove the soundness of Meursault's philosophy. But this is not enough. This comprehension is too purely intellectual, too negative, too superficial. It encloses the events in a philosophical skin.

Meursault intimates an affinity between his outlook and the "tender indifference" of the "universe." His indifference is the ataraxy of the sage. It lacks, but it permits, the penetration of tenderness—the alliance of the two words is paradoxical, but sound. It is Meursault's tenderness for what has happened that allows him to constitute his life as a destiny, to change contingency into existential necessity.

This tenderness, as well as this indifference, characterizes the tone of the narration. The narrator stands with the events, as well as above and after them. That is how I would justify the shifts to the present tense in the narration. Between the narrator and the narrated, there is a play of detachment and identification which echoes, and sometimes coincides with, the play between the aesthetic and the ethical elements. Thus the character catches up with the narrator in the final tableau: the confrontation with the starry night.

I have drawn an analogy between a star and a life seen in a perspective of exteriority. But Meursault says that he feels an affinity with the "universe," that is to say, with the spectacle as a whole. In this perspective, Meursault's life is not one life among others. His life is the ethical whole. The existential totalization which he effects finds its aesthetic analogue in the cosmic quality of the night. In this perspective of interiority, each star is analogous, not to one life, for instance Meursault's, but to one event in the life of Meursault.

To the priest who asks him how he would picture an after-life, Meursault answers: "A life in which I could remember this one." And on the last page I read: "I felt ready to live everything again." Is an "absurd" series of events worth remembering? Is it for the sake of proving his wisdom twice that Meursault feels ready to live this particular life again?

In life recollected, not in life lived moment after moment, totalization is possible and destiny may appear: this is the existential equivalent of a poem. In life lived again, not in life lived once, totalization would be possible from the start and destiny might appear: this would be the existential equivalent of a novel. As we read it, or perhaps reread it, the monologue of Meursault appears as the equivalent of a novel entitled *The Stranger*.

RENÉ GIRARD

Camus's Stranger Retried

We have always pictured Meursault as a stranger to the sentiments of other men. Love and hatred, ambition and envy, greed and jealousy are equally foreign to him. He attends the funeral of his mother as impassively as he watches, on the following day, a Fernandel movie. Eventually, Meursault kills a man, but how could we feel that he is a real criminal? How could this man have any motive for murder?

Meursault is the fictional embodiment of the nihilistic individualism expounded in *Le Mythe de Sisyphe* and commonly referred to as *l'absurde*. Meursault is possessed by this *absurde* as others, in a different spiritual context, are possessed by religious grace. But the word *absurde* is not really necessary; the author himself, in his preface to the Brée-Lynes edition of the novel, defines his hero as a man "who does not play the game." Meursault "refuses to lie" and, immediately, "society feels threatened." This hero has a positive significance, therefore; he is not an *épave*, a derelict; "he is a man poor and naked who is in love with the sun."

It is easy to oppose *L'Etranger* to a novel like *Crime and Punishment*. Dostoevsky *approves* the sentence that condemns his hero, whereas Camus *disapproves. L'Etranger* must be a work of innocence and generosity, soaring above the morass of a guilt-ridden literature. But the problem is not so simple as it looks. Meursault is not the only character in the novel. If he is

From "*To Double Business Bound*": *Essays on Literature, Mimesis, and Anthropology.* © 1978 by the Johns Hopkins University Press.

innocent, the judges who sentence him are guilty. The presentation of the trial as a parody of justice contains at least an implicit indictment of the judges. Many critics have made this indictment explicit and so has Camus himself in the preface to the American edition of *L'Etranger*. After presenting the death of his hero as the evil fruit of an evil collectivity, the author concludes: "In our society, a man who does not cry at the funeral of his mother is likely to be sentenced to death." This striking sentence is really a quotation from an earlier statement; it is labeled "paradoxical," but it is nevertheless repeated with the obvious intent to clear all possible misunderstanding as to an interpretation of *L'Etranger* that, in a sense, is beyond questioning.

La *Chute* was published in 1956, one year after the American edition of *L'Etranger*. In it, a fashionable Parisian lawyer named Clamence has made a great reputation defending those criminals whom he could, somehow, picture as victims of the "judges." Clamence has a very high opinion of himself because he has always sided with the "underdog" against the iniquitous "judges." One day, however, he discovers that moral heroism is not so easily achieved in deeds as it is in words, and a process of soul searching begins that leads the "generous lawyer" to abandon his successful career and take refuge in Amsterdam. Clamence realizes that mercy, in his hands, was a secret weapon against the unmerciful, a more complex form of self-righteousness. His real desire was not to save his clients but to prove his moral superiority by discrediting the judges. Clamence, in other words, had been the type of lawyer whom Salinger's hero, in *The Catcher in the Rye*, would hate to become:

> Lawyers are all right . . . if they go around saving innocent guys' lives all the time, and like that, but you don't *do* that kind of stuff if you're a lawyer. . . . And besides. Even if you *did* go around saving guys' lives, and all, how would you know if you did it because you really *wanted* to save guys' lives, or because what you *really* wanted to do was be a terrific lawyer, with everybody slapping you on the back and congratulating you in court when the goddam trial was over. . . . How would you know you weren't being a phony? The trouble is, you *wouldn't*.

The "generous lawyer" wants to be *above* everybody else and to sit in judgment over the judges themselves; he is a judge in disguise. Unlike the ordinary judges who judge directly and openly, he judges indirectly and deviously. When anti-Pharisaism is used as a device to crush the Pharisees, it becomes another and more vicious form of Pharisaism. This point is a pertinent one, especially in our time, but it is not new and it would not be so striking if Camus, in order to make it, did not return to the themes and symbols of his earlier works, in particular those of *L'Etranger*.

In *La Chute* as in *L'Etranger*, there are a court, a trial, the accused, and, of course, the inevitable judges. The only new character is the generous lawyer himself, who defends his "good criminals" just as Camus, the novelist, defended Meursault in *L'Etranger*. The good criminals lose their cases, and so did Meursault, but the loss, in either case, is more than regained in the wider court of public opinion. When we read *L'Etranger*, we feel pity for Meursault and anger with his judges, the very sentiments that the "generous lawyer" is supposed to derive from his practice of the law.

The pre-*Chute* Camus is quite different, of course, from his hero Clamence, but the two have a common trait in their contempt for the "judges." Both of them have built an intellectually complex and socially successful life around this one hallowed principle. The contemporary advocate of literary "revolt" is perpetually challenging social institutions and values, but his challenge, like that of the lawyer, has become a part of the institutions themselves; far from entailing any personal risks, his activities bring fame and comfort in their wake.

If Camus had conceived any doubts as to the validity of his ethical attitude and if he had wanted to express these doubts in another work of fiction, he could not have hit upon a more appropriate theme than that of *La Chute*. All the earlier works of the author are based upon the explicit or implicit tenet that a systematic hostility to all "judges" provides the surest foundation for an "authentic" ethical life. *La Chute* openly derides this tenet. It is natural, therefore, to conclude that the work contains an element of self-criticism. It is no less natural to reject a conclusion that threatens all established ideas concerning Camus, the writer and the man.

We live in an age of middle-class "individualism" in which self-consistency is rated as a major virtue. But a thinker is not bound by the same rules as a statesman or a banker. We do not think less of Goethe because he repudiated *Werther*. We do not blush at the thought of Rimbaud repudiating his whole work or of Kafka refusing to have his manuscripts published at the time of his death. Progress in matters of the spirit is often a form of self-destruction; it may entail a violent reaction against the past. If an artist has to keep admiring his own works at all times in order to remain admirable, Monsieur Joseph Prud'homme, the caricatural French bourgeois, is certainly greater than Pascal, Racine, Chateaubriand, or Claudel.

A writer's creative process has become a major, if not *the* major, literary theme of our time. The lawyer of *La Chute*, like the doctor of *La Peste*, is, at least to a certain extent, an allegory of the creator. Can this assertion be denied on the grounds that it involves a "naive confusion" between the author and his fictional work? Fear of the "biographical fallacy" must not be an excuse to evade the truly significant problems raised by literary creation. This fear is itself naive because it conceives of the rapport between an author and his work as an all-or-nothing proposition. When I say that Clamence *is* Albert Camus, I do not mean that the two are identical in the sense that an original document is identical to its carbon copy or that a traveler is identical to the snapshot that figures on the first page of his passport. When a work is really profound, the existential significance of its characters and situations can never be stated in terms of straight biography, but why should it have to be so stated?

I may admit that Camus's past is present in *La Chute* and still evade the most difficult consequences of this discovery. By placing the emphasis upon the political and social allusions, I may interpret the confession of Clamence as an attack against whatever is implied in the word *engagement*. Camus's quarrel with Sartre as well as his restrained public attitude during the last years of his life could provide some additional evidence for this view. If *La Chute* is a reaction against the recent past only, is it not, as such, a return to the earlier past and a vigorous—if enigmatic—restatement of the positions defended in *Sisyphe* and *L'Etranger*? This minimal interpretation is attractive; unfortunately, it rests not on internal evidence but on the implicit assumption that Camus's entire itinerary can and must be defined in terms of that *engagement/dégagement* polarity that reigned supreme a dozen years ago. The trouble with this polarity is that it excludes the one possibility that is actually realized in *La Chute*, that of a change in vision radical enough to transcend both the *engagement* of *La Peste* and the *dégagement* of *L'Etranger*.

Engagement can rarely be distinguished from the other targets of satire in *La Chute* because, from the standpoint of Clamence, it no longer constitutes a truly autonomous attitude. The first Camus, as well as the later advocate of *engagement*, can fit the description of the "generous lawyer." The only difference is that the "clients" are characters of fiction in the first case and real human beings in the second. From the cynical perspective of Clamence, this difference is unimportant. To the generous lawyer, the clients are never quite real since they are not an end in themselves, but they are never quite fictional since they are a means to discredit the judges. *Engagement* represents only a variation on the theme of "bad faith," one of the many forms that a secretly self-seeking dedication to the downtrodden can assume. Behind the clients, therefore, we can see the characters created by the early Camus, such as Caligula, the two women murderers in *Le Malentendu*, and, preeminently, Meursault no less than the real but shadowy people whose cause a writer is supposed to embrace when he becomes *engagé*.

The passage in which Clamence describes his kindness to old ladies in distress and other such people is probably the one direct reference to *engagement* in *La Chute*. And we may note that this boy-scoutish behavior is presented as nothing more than an extension of the lawyer's professional attitude. Clamence has become so engrossed in his legal self that he goes on playing the part of the generous lawyer outside of the court; the comedy gradually takes over even the most ordinary circumstances of daily life. Literature and life have become one, not because literature imitates life but because life imitates literature. Unity of experience is achieved at the level of an all-pervasive imposture.

La Chute must be read in the right perspective, which is one of humor. The author, tired of his popularity with all the *bien-pensants* of the intellectual élite, found a witty way to deride his quasiprophetic role without scandalizing the pure at heart among the faithful. Allowance must be made for overstatement, but the work cannot be discounted as a joke or safely extolled as art for art's sake. The confession of Clamence is Camus's own, in a broad literary and spiritual sense. To prove this point, I shall turn first to *L'Etranger* and uncover a structural flaw that, to my knowledge, has not been previously detected. The significance of that structural flaw will provide the evidence needed to confirm the reading of *La Chute* as self-criticism.

From a purely textual standpoint, Meursault's condemnation is almost unrelated to his crime. Every detail of the trial adds up to the conclusion that the judges resent the murderer not for what he did but for what he is. The critic Albert Maquet expressed this truth quite well when he wrote: "The murder of the Arab is only a pretext; behind the person of the accused, the judges want to destroy the truth he embodies."

Let there be no murder and a good pretext to get rid of Meursault will, indeed, have been lost, but a pretext should be easy to replace, precisely because it does not have to be good. If society is as eager to annihilate Meursault as it is pictured by Maquet, the remarkable existence of this hero should provide more "pretexts" than will ever be needed to send an innocent to his doom.

Is this assumption well founded? We ask this question in all awareness that we are abandoning, for the time being, pure textual analysis for common sense realism. If we feel, when we are reading the novel, that Meursault lives dangerously, this impression evaporates under examination. The man goes to work regularly; he swims on the beaches of the Mediterranean and he has dates with the girls in the office. He likes the movies but he is not interested in politics. Which of these activities will take him to a police station, let alone the guillotine?

Meursault has no responsibilities, no family, no personal problems; he feels no sympathy for unpopular causes. Apparently he drinks nothing but café au lait. He really lives the prudent and peaceful life of a little bureaucrat anywhere and of a French petit bourgeois in the bargain. He carries the fore-sight of his class so far that he waits the medically recommended number of hours after his noonday meal before he plunges into the Mediterranean. His way of life should constitute a good insurance against nervous breakdowns, mental exhaustion, heart failure, and, a fortiori, the guillotine.

Meursault, it is true, does not cry at his mother's funeral, and this is the one action in his life that is likely to be criticized by his neighbors; from such criticism to the scaffold, however, there is a distance that could never be bridged if Meursault did not commit a murder. Even the most ferocious judge could not touch a single hair on his head, had he not killed one of his fellow men.

The murder may be a pretext, but it is the only one available, and upon this unfortunate event, the whole structure of meaning erected by Camus comes to rest. It is very important, therefore, to understand how the murder comes to pass. How can a man commit a murder and not be responsible for it? The obvious answer is that this murder must be an *accident*, and many critics have taken up that answer. Louise Hudon, for instance, says that Meursault is guilty of involuntary manslaughter at worst. How could Meur-sault premeditate murder, since he cannot premeditate a successful career in Paris or marriage with his mistress? Involuntary manslaughter, as everyone knows, should not send a man to the guillotine. This interpretation seems to clinch Camus's case against the "judges."

There is a difficulty, however. If Meursault must commit a crime, we agree that he must be an involuntary rather than a voluntary criminal, but why should he commit a crime in the first place? Accidents will happen, no doubt, but no general conclusion can be drawn from them, or they cease, quite obviously, to be *accidents*. If the murder is an accident, so is the sentence that condemns Meursault, and *L'Etranger* does not prove that people who do not cry at their mothers' funerals are likely to be sentenced to death. All the novel proves, then, is that these people will be sentenced to death if they also happen to commit involuntary manslaughter, and this *if*, it will be conceded, is a very big one. The accident theory reduces Meur-sault's case to the proportions of a pathetic but rather insignificant *fait-divers*.

Let a million devotees of *l'absurde* copy Meursault's way of life down to the last dregs of his café au lait, let them bury their entire families without shedding a single tear, and not one of them will ever die on the guillotine, for the simple reason that their *imitatio absurdi* will not and should not include the accidental murder of the Arab; this unfortunate happening, in all proba-bility, will never be duplicated.

The accident theory weakens, if it does not destroy, the tragic opposition between Meursault and society. That is why it does not really account for the experience of the reader. Textually speaking, the relationship between Meursault and his murder cannot be expressed in terms of motivation, as would be the case with an ordinary criminal, but it is nevertheless felt to be essential, rather than accidental. From the very beginning of the novel we sense that something frightful is going to happen and that Meursault can do nothing to protect himself. The hero is innocent, no doubt, and this very innocence will bring about his downfall.

The critics who, like Carl Viggiani, have best captured the atmosphere of the murder reject all rational interpretations and attribute this event to that same *Fatum* that presides over the destinies of epic and tragic heroes in ancient and primitive literatures. They point out that the various incidents and objects connected with this episode can be interpreted as symbols of an implacable Nemesis.

We still invoke fate today when we do not want to ascribe an event to chance, even though we cannot account for it. This "explanation" is not meant seriously, however, when we are talking about real happenings taking place in the real world. We feel that this world is essentially rational and that it should be interpreted rationally.

An artist is entitled to disregard rational laws in his search for esthetic effects. No one denies this. If he makes use of this privilege, however, the world he creates is not only fictional but fantastic. If Meursault is sentenced to death in such a fantastic world, my indignation against the iniquitous judges must be fantastic too, and I cannot say, as Camus did in his preface to the Brée-Lynes edition of *L'Etranger*, that, *in our society*, people who behave like Meursault are likely to be sentenced to death. The conclusions that I infer from the novel are valid for this novel only and not for the real world, since the laws of verisimilitude have been violated. Meursault's drama does not give me the right to look with contempt upon real judges operating in a real court. Such contempt must be justified by a perfectly rational sequence of causes or motivations leading from the funeral of the mother to the death of the hero. If, at the most crucial point in this sequence, *Fatum* is suddenly brandished, or some other deity as vague as it is dark, we must note this is sudden disregard for the rational course of human affairs and take a very close look at the antisocial message of the novel.

If supernatural necessity is present in *L'Etranger*, why should Meursault alone come under its power? Why should the various characters in the same novel be judged by different yardsticks? If the murderer is not held responsible for his actions, why should the judges be held responsible for theirs? It is possible, of course, to read part of *L'Etranger* as fantasy and the rest as realistic fiction, but the novel thus fragmented presents no unified world view; even from a purely esthetic point of view it is open to criticism.

The fate theory looks satisfactory as long as the episode of the murder remains detached from the novel, but it cannot be integrated with this novel. Sympathy for Meursault is inseparable from resentment against the judges. We cannot do away with that resentment without mutilating our global esthetic experience. This resentment is really generated by the text, and we must somehow account for it even if it is not logically justified.

The search for the significance of Meursault's murderous gesture leads nowhere. The death of the Arab can be neither an accident nor an event inspired from "above," and yet it must be one of these two things if it is not voluntary. It is as difficult to ascribe an "ontological status" to the murder as it is easy to ascertain its function in the story. Meursault, as I have said, could never have been tried, convicted, and sentenced if he had not killed the Arab. But Camus thought otherwise, and he said so in the preface to *L'Etranger*: "A man who does not cry at the funeral of his mother is likely to be sentenced to death." Is this an a posteriori judgment deduced from the facts of the story, as everybody has always taken for granted, or is it an a priori principle to which the "facts" must somehow be fitted? Everything becomes intelligible if we choose the second solution. Camus needs his "innocent murder" because his a priori principle is blatantly false. The irritating cult of motherhood and the alleged profundities of *l'absurde* must not obscure the main issue. Let us translate the brilliant paradoxes of the author back into the terms of his story, let us remove the halo of intellectual sophistication that surrounds the novel, and no one will take its message seriously. Do we really believe that the French judicial system is ruthlessly dedicated to the extermination of little bureaucrats addicted to café au lait, Fernandel movies, and casual love affairs with the boss's secretary?

One of the reasons we do not question the tragic ending of *L'Etranger* is the lowly status of its hero. Little clerks are, indeed, potential and actual victims of our modern societies. Like the other members of his class, Meursault is vulnerable to a multitude of social ills ranging from war to racial and economic discrimination. But this fact, on close examination, has no bearing on Camus's tragedy. The work is not one of social but of individual protest, even though the author welcomes the ambiguity, or at least does nothing to dispel it. The main point is that Meursault is the incarnation of unique qualities rather than the member of a group. The judges are supposed to resent what is most Meursault-like in Meursault. Unfortunately, the alleged uniqueness of this hero has no concrete consequences in his behavior. For all practical purposes, Meursault is a little bureaucrat devoid of ambition and, as such, he cannot be singled out for persecution. The only real threats to his welfare are those he shares with every other little bureaucrat, or with the human race as a whole.

The idea of the novel is incredible; that is why a direct demonstration is unthinkable. The writer wanted to arouse an indignation that he himself felt, and he had to take into account the demands of elementary realism. In order to become a martyr, Meursault had to commit some truly reprehensible action, but in order to retain the sympathy of the readers, he had to remain innocent. His crime had to be involuntary, therefore, but not so involuntary that the essential Meursault, the man who does not cry at his mother's funeral, would remain untouched by the sentence. All the events leading to the actual scene of the shooting, including that scene itself, with its first involuntary shot followed by four voluntary ones, are so devised that they appear to fulfill these two incompatible exigencies. Meursault will die an innocent, and yet his death sentence will be more significant than a mere judicial error.

This solution is really no solution at all. It can only hide, it cannot resolve, the contradiction between the first and the second Meursault, between the peaceful solipsist and the martyr of society; it *is* that contradiction in a nutshell, as revealed by the two conflicting words, "innocent" and "murder," whose combination sounds unusual and interesting, somewhat like a surrealistic image, precisely because they cannot form a real concept and be fused together any more than a surrealistic image can evoke a real object.

The skillful narrative technique makes it very difficult to perceive the logical flaw in the structure of the novel. When an existence as uneventful as that of Meursault is described in minute detail, without any humor, an atmosphere of tense expectation is automatically created. As I read the novel, my attention is focused upon details that are insignificant in themselves but that come to be regarded as portents of doom just because the writer has seen fit to record them. I sense that Meursault is moving toward a tragedy, and this impression, which has nothing to do with the hero's actions, seems to arise from them. Who can see a woman knitting alone in a dark house at the beginning of a mystery story without being led to believe that knitting is a most dangerous occupation?

In the second half of *L'Etranger*, all the incidents recorded in the first half are recalled and used as evidence against Meursault. The aura of fear that surrounds these incidents appears fully justified. We are aware of these trifles as trifles but we have been conditioned to regard them as potentially dangerous to the hero. It is natural, therefore, to consider the attitude of the judges both unfair and inevitable. In a mystery story, the clues ultimately lead to the murderer; in *L'Etranger*, they all lead to the judges. The murder itself

is handled in the same casual and fateful manner as the other actions of
Meursault. Thus, the gap between this portentous action and an afternoon
swim in the Mediterranean or the absorption of a cup of café au lait is gradually narrowed, and we are gently led to the incredible conclusion that the
hero is sentenced to death not for the crime of which he is accused and that
he has really committed, but for his innocence, which this crime has not
tarnished and which should remain obvious to all people at all times, as if it
were the attribute of a divinity.

   L'Etranger was not written for pure art's sake, nor was it written to
vindicate the victims of persecution everywhere. Camus set out to prove that
the hero according to his heart will necessarily be persecuted by society. He
set out to prove, in other words, that "the judges are always in the wrong."
The truth deeply buried in *L'Etranger* would have been discovered long
before it became explicit in *La Chute* if we had read the tragedy of Meursault
with truly critical eyes. A really close reading leads, indeed, to questioning
the structure and, beyond it, the "authenticity" of *L'Etranger* in terms identical with those of Clamence's confession. The allegory of the generous
lawyer stems from the structural flaw of *L'Etranger*, fully apprehended for the
first time and interpreted as the "objective correlative" of the author's "bad
faith." Further evidence can be provided by the explication of some obscure
passages and apparent contradictions in the text of *La Chute*.

   Here is a first example. At one point in the description of his past professional life Clamence remarks: "Je ne me trouvais pas sur la scène du tribunal
mais quelque part, dans les cintres, comme ces dieux que, de temps en temps,
on descend, au moyen d'une machine, pour transfigurer l'action et lui donner
un sens." Readers acquainted with the terminology of postwar French criticism
will remember that Sartre and his school accuse novelists of mistaking themselves for "gods" when they warp the destiny of a character and when,
consciously or not, they lead him to some preordained conclusion. If we recognize the figure of the writer behind the mask of the lawyer we shall immediately perceive, in this bizarre statement, an allusion, and a very pertinent one,
to the wrong kind of novelist. Can this same statement be made meaningful if
La Chute is not understood as an allegory of the writer's own literary past?

   The image of the god is originally Sartrian, but the Greek element
brings us back to those critics who have rejected all rational interpretation of
the murder. They themselves are solely concerned with problems of esthetic
symbolism, but their writings may well have helped Camus realize what he
now implicitly denounces as the "bad faith" of his own creation. The murder
of the Arab, in a novel otherwise rational and realistic, is a *deus ex machina*,
or rather a *crimen ex machina* that provides the author not with a happy
ending but with a tragic one that is really precluded by the character he
himself has given to his hero.

Here is a second example. Clamence tells us that he chose his clients "à la seule condition qu'ils fussent de bons meurtriers comme d'autres de bons sauvages." This sentence is absolutely unintelligible in a nonliterary context. It is a thinly disguised reference to Meursault, who plays, in his fictional world, a role similar to that of the good savage, a well-known pre-Romantic stranger, in the world of eighteenth-century literature. Here again, the image may have been suggested by Sartre, who, in his *Situations* article, defined *L'Etranger* as a twentieth-century *conte philosophique*.

Like the "bon sauvage," Meursault is supposed to act as a catalyst; his sole presence reveals the arbitrariness of the values that bind the "insiders" together. The *bonté* of this abstract figure is an absolute that no amount of *sauvagerie* can diminish. Meursault's excellence has the same quality. He is no less innocent and the judges no less guilty for punishing him, a confessed criminal, than if no crime had been committed. Innocence and guilt are fixed essences; they cannot be affected by the vicissitudes of existence any more than Ormazd and Ahriman can exchange their roles as the principle of good and the principle of evil.

In *La Chute*, the author questions his own motives for writing fiction within the framework of this fiction itself. Meursault, as a "client" of Clamence, has retreated in the background and become anonymous, but he is still a dramatis persona, and the structural incoherence of *L'Etranger* must be expressed primarily in terms of *his* personal motivations. In order to denounce what he now regards as his own moral illusions and creative weakness, Clamence must say, as he does, that *his clients were not so innocent after all*. Their allegedly spontaneous and unmotivated misdeeds were, in fact, premeditated. If Camus is to abide by the rules of the fictional game initiated in the first novel, he must attribute to the hero the "bad faith" that really belongs to his creator, and this is precisely what he does. The "good criminals" killed, not for any of the ordinary reasons, as we are well aware, but because they *wanted* to be tried and sentenced. Clamence tells us that their motives were really the same as his: like so many of our contemporaries, in this anonymous world, they wanted a little publicity.

Meursault, however, is a character of fiction; responsibility for his crime lies, in the last resort, with the creator himself. The present reading would be more convincing if Clamence, instead of placing the blame upon his "clients," had placed it squarely upon himself. But Clamence is already the lawyer; how could he be the instigator of the crime without absurdity? Such transparent allegory would deal the last blow to *La Chute* as art for art's sake and the present exegesis would be pointless. Let me apologize, therefore, for belaboring the obvious since Clamence does, indeed, present himself both as the passionate defender and as the accomplice of his good criminals. He does not hesitate to assume these two incompatible roles. If we reject the obvious implications of this inconstistency, we must dare condemn *La Chute* as an incoherent piece of fiction.

This is a curious lawyer, indeed, who manipulates the court from high above, as he would a puppet show, and who discovers the guilt of his clients *after* they are sentenced, even though he himself had a hand in their crimes. We must observe, on the other hand, that this collusion with the criminals should destroy the image of the generous lawyer as a stuffy, self-righteous, upper-middle-class man if the reader did not realize, subconsciously at least, that these criminals are only paper ones. The account of Clamence's law career is really a collection of metaphors, all pointing to "unauthentic creation," and Camus uses them as he sees fit, tearing as he goes the thin veil of his fiction. Clamence really suggests that the author of *L'Etranger* was not really conscious of his own motivation until he experienced his own *chute*. His purpose, which disguised itself as "generosity," was really identical with egotistical passion. *L'Etranger* must not be read as a *roman à thèse*. The author did not consciously try to deceive his audience, but he succeeded all the better because he managed to deceive himself in the first place. The dichotomy between Meursault and his judges represents the dichotomy between the Self and the Others in a world of intersubjecitve warfare.

L'Etranger, as the expression of egotistical values and meanings, forms a structure, a relatively stable "world view." Camus "sincerely" believed in his and, consequently, in Meursault's innocence, because he passionately believed in the guilt of the "judges." The incoherence of the plot does not stem from an awkward effort to prove something that was only half believed or not believed at all. On the contrary, the author's conviction that the iniquity of the judges can always be proved was so strong that nothing could shake it. The innocent will inevitably be treated as a criminal. In the process of proving this point, Camus had to turn his innocent into a real criminal, but his faith was such that he did not perceive the tautology. We can understand, now, why the "generous lawyer" is presented to us both as the sincere defender of his clients and as the accomplice of their crimes.

As long as the egotistical Manicheism that produced *L'Etranger* held its sway over him, the author could not perceive the structural flaw of his novel. All illusions are one. They stand together and they fall together as soon as their cause, egotistical passion, is perceived. The confession of Clamence does not lead to a new "interpretation" of *L'Etranger* but to an act of transcendence; the perspective of this first novel is rejected.

The rejection of the world view expressed in *L'Etranger* is not the fruit of an empirical discovery but of an existential conversion, and it is, indeed, such a conversion that is described ironically but unmistakably throughout the novel, in terms of an ego-shattering *chute*. This spiritual metamorphosis is triggered, so to speak, by the incident of the drowning woman but, basically, it has nothing to do with exterior circumstances. Neither can our own reevaluation of *L'Etranger* in the light of *La Chute* rest on external evidence such as scholarly arguments and "explications de textes," however massive the material proof available through these channels. The evidence will not be judged convincing until there is a willingness to go along with the self-critical mood of the creator. I, the reader, must undergo an experience, less profound to be sure, but somewhat analogous to that of this creator. The true critic must not remain superbly and coldly objective; he is the one most profoundly affected and transformed by the work of art; he truly *sympathizes*, suffers with the author. I, too, must fall from my pedestal; as an admirer of *L'Etranger*, I must accept the risk of an exegetical *chute*.

A refusal to probe the confession of Clamence must not be rationalized on the grounds that it makes the literary reputation of Camus more secure. It is the reverse that is true. The fact that *La Chute* transcends the perspective of *L'Etranger* does not mean that, in a comparison with other works of recent fiction, the earlier work ranks lower than had been previously thought; it certainly means, however, that *La Chute* ranks higher.

A gingerly approach to *La Chute* obscures the true greatness of Camus. This work can already be defined as a forgotten masterpiece. Camus is praised to the high heavens by some, while others deride his role as "directeur de conscience" of the middle class, but all this is done with only passing reference, or no reference at all, to *La Chute*. Most people ignore the fact that Albert Camus was the first one to react against his own cult. Here and there, some voices are raised in defense of a truth that no one, it seems, is really eager to hear. Philippe Sénart, for instance, maintained that Camus refused to be the infallible pope of his own new neohumanism:

> Il ne voulait être que le *pape des fous* et il écrivait *La Chute* pour se tourner en dérision et il s'accusait en se moquant. Clamence, avocat déchu, qui avait "bien vécu de sa vertu," qui se trouvait, avec coquetterie, "un peu surhomme," était, dans le bouge où il se déguisait en juge pour mieux rire de lui, le Bouffron de l'humanité, d'aucuns disaient le Singe de Dieu, comme Satan. Clamence, l'Homme-qui-rit, c'était l'Anti-Camus.

In one of the speeches pronounced when he received his Nobel Prize, Camus opened still a new line of investigation to the critics of his work:

> Le thème du poète maudit né dans une société marchande (Chatterton en est la plus belle illustration), s'est durci dans un préjugé qui finit par vouloir qu'on ne puisse être un grand artiste que

> contre la société de son temps, quelle qu'elle soit. Légitime à son
> origine quand il affirmait qu'un artiste véritable ne pouvait
> composer avec le monde de l'argent, le principe est devenu faux
> lorsqu'on en a tiré qu'un artiste ne pouvait s'affirmer qu'en étant
> contre toute chose en général.

Throughout the *Discours de Suède*, Camus dissociated himself from his own past as much as the occasion permitted. Here, he relates the type of literature he himself had practiced for so long not to an awe-inspiring philosophical tradition, as in *L'Homme révolté*, but to French Romanticism. He chooses as the archetype of *révolté*, *Chatterton*, the one work of Alfred de Vigny with which contemporary readers are likely to find most fault. He suggests that the tragic conflicts set forth in his own early works are really a *degraded* form of Vigny's Romantic drama.

An earlier Camus would certainly have rejected this rapprochement out of hand in spite or rather because of its extreme relevance. *L'Etranger* is really much closer to *Chatterton* than to the *conte philosophique* because the *conte* has a concrete content and it fights for definite objectives, whereas *Chatterton*, like *L'Etranger*, is primarily an abstract protest of the discontented ego. A work that is against everything in general is really against nothing in particular and no one actually feels disturbed by it. Like Dostoevsky's underground man, Meursault says: "I am alone and *they* are together." The work spells the final democratization of the Romantic myth, the universal symbol of the separated ego in a world where almost everyone feels like an "outsider."

Chatterton, like Meursault, was conceived as a lonely figure, as a man who refuses "to play the game." Both men live in a world of their own that contrasts with the unauthentic world of other men. Both of them suffer and die because society makes it impossible for them to live according to their own lonely, infinitely superior ways.

There is a difference, however. When Chatterton is offered the same type of third-rate job Meursault holds, he refuses haughtily. In his eyes, this menial way of life is incompatible with his mission. We find it rather easy to interpret Chatterton's destiny in terms of Romantic pride. Camus's hero appears very humble by contrast; he does not view himself as a man with a mission; he has no visible pretensions and he is ready to do whatever is necessary to sustain his mediocre existence.

This modest appearance really hides a more extreme form of Romantic pride. Between Chatterton and other men there is still a measure of reciprocity, whereas none is left in the case of Meursault. Chatterton gives his "genius" and the community must give him food and shelter in return. If society does not fulfill its share of the contract, the poet cannot fulfill his role as a great poet; the crowd grows spiritually hungry and the poet grows physically hungry. This general starvation is less tragic, no doubt, than Greek or classical tragedy and it is so because Chatterton is less deeply involved with his fellowmen than earlier tragic heroes. Real tragedy demands genuine involvement. It is somewhat ironic, let us note in passing, that a doctrine with such ethereal pretensions as 1830 Romanticism could produce only alimentary tragedies of the Chatterton type. But this last meager resource is still truly present, whereas it is gone in the case of Camus. The poetic life cherished by Chatterton has become a part of the shameful game that the real individual must refuse to play in order to remain "authentic." *L'Etranger* should not end in a Chatterton-like tragedy; it should revolve around the closed circle of a perfectly self-sufficient personality. An endless succession of cafés au lait, Fernandel movies, and amorous interludes should provide a scale model of the Nietzschean eternal return.

Romantic pride separates Chatterton from his fellowmen; greater pride cuts Meursault off so completely that no tragic possibilities remain. In order to grasp this point, we may compare Meursault with another Romantic in disguise, Monsieur Teste, the solipsistic hero of Valéry's youth. Monsieur Teste is infinitely brilliant and original but he alone is aware of his own worth. He is satisfied, like Meursault, with a third-rate job; he does not mind looking *quelconque* and remaining unknown. He will never be a *grand homme* because he refuses to sacrifice anything to the spirit of the crowd. Meursault is really a Teste without a Ph.D., a Teste who prefers café au lait to higher mathematics, a super-Teste, in other words, who does not even bother to be intelligent.

The idea of turning Teste into a martyr of society would have sounded ludicrous to Valéry. The only thing a solipsist is entitled to ask of society is indifference, and indifference he will get if he behaves like a Teste or a Meursault. Valéry was perfectly aware that, as individualism becomes more extreme, the possibilities offered to a writer shrink; and he rejected as "impure" all types of dramatic literature.

L'Etranger begins like *Monsieur Teste* and it ends like *Chatterton*. Unlike Valéry, Camus does not perceive or he refuses to assume the consequences of his literary solipsism. He resorts to the device of the "innocent murder" in order to retrieve the structure of the *poète maudit* or, more generally, of the "exceptional man persecuted by society." The *crimen ex machina* saves the author from the limitations of his own attitude.

Contemporary readers sense that there is something contrived in *Chatterton*, and yet Vigny did not have to turn his exceptional man into a murderer in order to present him as a martyr of society. *L'Etranger* should appear even more contrived, but we do not understand the disturbing role that violence plays in it, probably because the novel is the latest successful formulation of the myth of the Romantic self.

Chatterton already prefers to be persecuted rather than ignored, but we cannot prove the point because it is plausible that society will prevent a poet from fulfilling his destiny as a poet. In the case of Meursault, this same preference for egotistical martyrdom can be proven, because it is not plausible that society will prevent a little bureaucrat from fulfilling his destiny as a little bureaucrat. Camus takes his hero out of society with one hand only to put him back with the other. He wants Meursault to be a solipsist, then turns him into the hero of a trial, that quintessence of diseased human relations in our modern society.

Why does Camus crave solitude and society at the same time; why is he both repelled and fascinated by *les autres?* The contradiction is really inherent in the Romantic personality. The Romantic does not want to be alone, but *to be seen alone.* In *Crime and Punishment,* Dostoevsky shows that solitary dreams and the "trial" are the two inseparable facets, the dialectically related "moments" of the Romantic consciousness. But this proud consciousness refuses to acknowledge openly the fascination it feels for the others. In the days of Vigny a discreet return to society was still possible because a few bridges were left between the individualist and his fellowmen. The "mission of the poet" was one, romantic love another. Camus has destroyed these last bridges because the urge to be alone is stronger in him than ever before. But the unacknowledged urge to return to other men is also stronger than ever. And this second urge can no longer be satisfied within the context created by the first.

The murder is really a secret effort to reestablish contact with humanity. It reveals an ambivalence that is present in all art with solipsistic tendencies but that has probably never been so visibly written into the structure of a work. This contradiction is also present in *Monsieur Teste* because it can never be eliminated completely. Monsieur Teste lives and dies alone, but not so much alone that we, the readers, are left in the dark about his superhuman and invisible qualities. The egotistical *Deus* is never so *absconditus* that it does not have its priests and mediators. The ambiguous narrator plays the part of the "innocent murder" in *L'Etranger.* He is an artificial bridge between the solipsist and ordinary mortals. He is close enough to Teste to understand him and close enough to us to write for us. Such a man, by definition, should not exist and the work should never have been written. Valéry was so aware of it that he remained silent for twenty years after writing *Monsieur Teste.*

Camus, too, should be silent and he is at least partly aware of it since, in *Sisyphe,* he discusses literature and concludes that it is a fitting pastime for the knight-errant of *l'absurde*—provided, of course, it is not oriented to *les autres*. This a posteriori justification must be read primarily as evidence that the problem was a significant and important one for Camus at the time. The pure doctrine of solipsism is not in *Sisyphe* but in *L'Etranger*. Meursault does not read or write; we cannot imagine him submitting a manuscript to a publisher or correcting galley proofs. All such activities have no place in an "authentic" existence.

Both the young Valéry and the young Camus cherished literature; both knew that it offered an avenue of escape from their equally mediocre stations in life. And yet both of them held views that made the practice of their art almost impossible. Romantic individualism becomes so exacerbated with these writers that it verges on a certain type of neurotic behavior.

We all know, outside of literature, that certain people are too proud to acknowledge a situation as painful. These people may even do their utmost to perpetuate or even aggravate this situation in order to prove to themselves that it is *freely chosen*. The creation of Meursault certainly reflects an attitude of this type. The life of this hero is objectively sad and sordid. The man is, indeed, a derelict; he has no intellectual life, no love, no friendship, no interest in anyone or faith in anything. His life is limited to physical sensations and to cheap pleasures of modern mass culture. The uninformed readers—American undergraduates, for instance—often perceive this essential wretchedness; they grasp the *objective* significance of the novel because the *subjective* intention of the creator escapes them. The "informed" reader, on the other hand, rejects the objective significance as naive because he readily perceives the subjective intention, and he feels very sophisticated—until he reads and understands *La Chute*. Clamence alone is aware that there are two layers of significance, subjective and objective, and he picks the latter as the essential one when he states that his "good criminals" were wretched people *at bottom*. The most lucid view justifies the most naive; the truth belongs to the reader who takes *nothing* or *everything* into account, and to no one in between.

The undergraduates quickly learn, of course, that it is not smart to pity Meursault, but they vaguely wonder, for a while, why his living hell should be interpreted as paradise. This hell is the one to which, rightly or wrongly, Camus felt condemned in the years of *L'Etranger*. There are psychological, social, and even metaphysical reasons, as well as literary ones, for *L'Etranger*'s mood of repressed despair. These were troubled times; opportunity was scarce; the health of the young Camus was not good; he was not yet a famous writer and he had no assurance that he would ever become one. He *willed*, therefore, as many did who came before and after him, the solitude and mediocrity from which he did not see any escape. His was an act of intellectual pride and desperation reminiscent of Nietzschean *amor fati*. Valéry's

Monsieur Teste stems from a comparable experience in a world somewhat less harsh. A young man who feels doomed to anonymity and mediocrity is compelled to repay with indifference the indifference of society. If he is very gifted, he may devise a new and radical variety of Romantic solipsism; he may create a Teste or a Meursault.

Even more relevant here than a purely psychiatric interpretation are the passages of *The Sickness unto Death* dedicated to what Kierkegaard calls "defiance," or "the despair of willing despairingly to be oneself."

> This too is a form of despair: not to be willing to hope that an earthly distress, a temporal cross, might be removed. This is what the despair which wills desperately to be itself is not willing to hope. It has convinced itself that this thorn in the flesh gnaws so profoundly that he cannot abstract in—no matter whether this is actually so or his passion makes it true for him—and so he is willing to accept it as it were eternally. So he is offended by it, or rather from it he takes occasion to be offended at the whole of existence. . . . To hope in the possibility of help, not to speak of help by virtue of the absurd, that for God all things are possible— no, that he will not do. And as for seeking help from any other— no, that he will not do for all the world; rather than seek help he would prefer to be himself—with all the torture of hell, if so must be. . . . Now it is too late, he once would have given everything to be rid of this torment but was made to wait, now that's all past, now he would rather rage against everything, he, the one man in the whole of existence who is the most unjustly treated, to whom it is especially important to have his torment at hand, important that no one should take it from him—for thus he can convince himself that he is in the right.

The absurd of which Kierkegaard is speaking, needless to say, is not Camus's *absurde*. It is rather the opposite of it, since it is the final rejection of nihilism, rejected by Camus himself and dismissed as facile optimism in *Sisyphe*. The young Camus thought he could dispose of Kierkegaard in a few sentences but Kierkegaard on Camus goes much deeper, paradoxically, than Camus on Kierkegaard: "such self-control, such firmness, such ataraxia, etc., border almost on the fabulous. . . . The self wants . . . to have the honor of this poetical, this masterly plan according to which it has understood itself. And yet, . . . just at the instant when it seems to be nearest to having the fabric finished it can arbitrarily resolve the whole thing into nothing."

This highest form of despair, Kierkegaard informs us, is encountered solely in the works of a few great poets, and we perceive the bond between the Vigny of *Chatterton*, the Valéry of *Teste*, and the Camus of *L'Etranger* when the philosopher adds: "one might call it Stoicism—yet without thinking only of this philosophic sect." The genius of Kierkegaard cuts through the maze of minor differences that help a writer assert his own individuality, thus obscuring the fundamental significance of his literary posture. The whole spiritual structure is grasped through a single act of intuition. The essential features are revealed, common, as a rule, to two or more writers. The following passage enables us, for instance, to account for the similarities between Teste and Meursault:

> One might represent the lower forms of despair by describing or by saying something about the outward traits of the depairer. But the more despair becomes spiritual, and the more is the self alert with demoniac shrewdness to keep despair shut up in close reserve, and all the more intent therefore to set the outward appearance at the level of indifference, to make it as unrevealing and indifferent as possible. . . . This hiddenness is precisely something spiritual and is one of the safety devices for assuring oneself of having as it were behind reality an enclosure, a world for itself locking all else out, a world where the despairing self is employed as tirelessly as Tantalus in willing to be itself.

This last reference might as well be to Sisyphus rather than to Tantalus. Camus's *Sisyphe*, like *Teste*, is a "rationalization" of Kierkegaardian despair, whereas *L'Etranger* is the esthetic, or naive and, as such, most revealing expression of that same despair.

Here again, we must not let the hollow specter of the "biographical fallacy" interfere with our comprehension of an author's fundamental problems. We do not confuse the creator with his creation. The relationship is not a simple one. Meursault is the portrait, or even the caricature, of a man Camus never was but swore to be, at the end of his adolescence, because he feared he could never be anyone else. The scene with the employer is revelatory. Meursault, as we all know, is offered a trip to Paris and the possibility of a permanent job there. He is not interested. The incident has only one purpose, which is to demonstrate Meursault's total lack of ambition. And it does what it is supposed to do; it does it, in a sense, too well; it is just a little too pointed. Why should *any* little clerk with a penchant for sun bathing want to move to Paris, with its dreary winter climate? At the lower echelon, which is Meursault's, sunny Algeria offers the same possibilities for advancement as the French capital. As Meursault refuses, with studied indifference, to live in Saint-Germain-des-Prés, we can hear Camus himself protesting that he has no literary ambitions.

Camus left Algeria for Paris; he wrote and published quite a few books; he submitted, at least for a few years, to the various indignities that the fabrication of a *grand homme* demands. The conclusion is inescapable: Camus, unlike his hero, was not devoid of ambition, especially literary ambition. This truth is as obvious as it is innocuous, but it sounds almost blasphemous; we are still living in the atmosphere of puritanical egotism that fosters such works as *L'Etranger* and that prevents us from reading them critically.

The urge to escape solitude was stronger than the self-destructive dynamism of repressed pride. But this urge had to prevail in an underhanded fashion. Camus could not contradict himself too openly. The style of the novel reveals how he managed to deceive himself. Rhetorical ornaments are systematically avoided; the author uses none of the gestures that serve to emphasize a good point. We feel that he is not looking at us and that he hardly unclenches his teeth. He rejects even the affectation of vulgarity and profanity that the preceding generation had adopted in an earlier attempt to destroy rhetoric—with the sole result, of course, of creating a new one. The famous rejection of the preterite—or of the present—the two tenses of formal narration, for the *passé composé* that is a conversational tense, amounts to an abandonment of all approved techniques of story telling. The author refuses to be a *raconteur* who performs for an audience. His *écriture blanche* gives an effect of greyish monotony that is the next best thing to silence, and silence is the only conduct truly befitting a solipsist, the only one, however, that he cannot bring himself to adopt.

This style bears a striking resemblance to the style of Meursault's actions prior to the murder. We feel that someone, on some fine day, handed Camus a pen and a piece of paper and Camus did the natural and mechanical thing to do, in such circumstances, which is to start writing, just as Meursault did the natural and mechanical thing to do, when you receive a gun, which is to start shooting. The book, like the murder, appears to be the result of fortuitous circumstances. The overall impression is that *L'Etranger* was written in the same bored, absentminded, and apathetic fashion as the Arab was murdered. We have a crime and we have no criminal; we have a book and we have no writer.

Camus and his hero have sworn to forsake all but the most superficial contacts with their fellowmen. Overtly, at least, they both kept their oaths. Meursault refused to go to Paris; Camus criticized writers and thinkers naive enough to believe in communication. But the oath was not kept so firmly that Meursault refrained from killing the Arab or Camus from writing *L'Etranger*. A murder and a book are not superficial contacts but, in the case of the murder, the destructive nature of the contact as well as the casual way in which it was obtained make it possible to deny that there is any contact at all.

Similarly, the antisocial nature of the book, as well as the furtive nature of its creation, make it possible to deny that the solipsist is really appealing to other men.

Camus betrays solipsism when he writes *L'Etranger* just as Meursault betrays it when he murders the Arab. The close analogy between the murder of the Arab and the style of the novel is not difficult to explain; every aspect of the work bears the imprint of a single creative act that stands in the same relation to its own consequence, the book, as Meursault's behavior to his murder. The "innocent murder" is really the image and the crux of the whole creative process. Clamence is aware of that fact when he insists that he, as a lawyer, had the same hidden motives as his clients. He, too, craved publicity but he did not have to pay as dearly as the actual criminals for the satisfaction of that impure desire. He should have shared in the punishment as he had shared in the crime, but he was acclaimed, instead, as a great moral leader:

> Le crime tient sans trêve le devant de la scène, mais le criminel n'y figure que fugitivement pour être aussitôt remplacé. Ces brefs triomphes enfin se paient trop cher. Défendre nos malheureux aspirants à la réputation revenait, au contraire, à être vraiment reconnu, dans le même temps et aux mêmes places, mais par des moyens plus économiques. Cela m'encourageait aussi à déployer de méritoires efforts pour qu'ils payassent le moins possible; ce qu'ils payaient, ils le payaient un peu à ma place.

Camus does not want us to believe that his motives, as a writer, were those of a literary opportunist writing cheap best sellers. From the higher standpoint of *La Chute*, he realizes that his own involvement in the tragic conflicts represented in his work was rooted in his own ambitions and in that stubborn need for self-justification to which we all succumb. *L'Etranger* is a real work of art since it can be apprehended as a single structure; its stylistic features are reflected in its plot and vice versa. We must not speak of the novel's *unity*, however, but of its consistent duality and of its radical ambiguity. How could the novel be one when its creative process is truly "divided against itself"? Every page of the work reflects the contradiction and the division inherent in the murder; every denial of communication is really an effort to communicate; every gesture of indifference or hostility is an appeal in disguise. The critical perspective suggested by *La Chute* illuminates even those structural elements that the esthetic approach makes its essential concern but that it ultimately leaves out of account because it isolates them from the content of the work and its many-sided significance.

Can we really understand the murder of the Arab, the structure of the novel, its style, and the "inspiration" of the novelist as a single process? We can if we compare this process to certain types of immature behavior. Let us imagine a child who, having been denied something he wanted very much, turns away from his parents; no blandishments will make him come out of his retreat. Like Meursault, like the first Camus, this child manages to convince himself that his sole desire is to be left alone.

If the child is left alone, his solitude quickly becomes unbearable but pride prevents him from returning meekly to the family circle. What can he do, then, to reestablish contact with the outside world? He must commit an action that will force the attention of the adults but that will not be interpreted as abject surrender, a *punishable* action, of course. But an overt challenge would still be too transparent; the punishable action must be committed covertly and deviously. The child must affect toward the instruments of his future misdeed the same casual attitude as Meursault toward his crime or as Camus toward literature.

Look at Meursault: he starts mingling with underworld characters inadvertently and casually, just as he would associate with anyone else; the matter is of no real consequence since other people do not really exist for him. Meursault, gradually, becomes involved in the shady dealings of his associates but he is hardly aware of this involvement. Why should he care, since one action is as good as another? The child's behavior is exactly the same; he picks up, for instance, a box of matches; he plays with it for a while, absent-mindedly; he does not mean any harm, of course, but all of a sudden, a match is aflame, and the curtains too if they happen to be nearby. Is it an *accident* or is it *fate*? It is "bad faith" and the child feels, like Meursault, that he is not responsible. Objects, to him, are mere fragments of substance lost in a chaotic universe. The *absurde*, in the sense popularized by *Sisyphe*, has become incarnate in this child.

L'Etranger was written and is usually read from the warped perspective that has just been defined. The secretly provocative nature of the murder is never acknowledged and the reprisals of society are presented as unprovoked aggression. The relationship between the individual and society is thereby turned upside down; a lonely individual, Meursault, is presented as completely indifferent to the collectivity, whereas the collectivity is supposed to be intensely concerned with his daily routine. This picture is false, and we all know it. Indifference really belongs to the collectivity; intense concern should be the lot of the lonely and miserable hero. The real picture is found in the few truly great works of fiction of Cervantes, Balzac, Dickens, Dostoeveksy, and, we might add, the Camus of *La Chute*.

The truth denied in *L'Etranger* is really so overwhelming that it comes out almost openly at the end of the novel, in Meursault's passionate outburst of resentment. Many readers have rightly felt that this conclusion rings more true than the rest of the novel. The resentment was there all along but pride silenced it, at least until the death sentence, which gave Meursault a pretext to express his despair without losing face in his own estimation. The child, too, wants to be punished, in order to express his grief without confessing its real cause, even to himself. In the last sentence, Meursault practically acknowledges that the sole and only guillotine threatening him is the indifference of *les autres*. *"Pour que tout soit consommé, pour que je me sente moins seul, il me restait à souhaiter qu'il y ait beaucoup de spectateurs le jour de mon exécution et qu'ils m'accueillent avec des cris de haine."*

The structural flaw in *L'Etranger* becomes intelligible when the novel is assimilated to a type of behavior that has become very common, even among adults, in our contemporary world. Meursault's empty life, his sullen mood, his upside-down world, no less than his half-hearted and secretly provocative crime, are typical of what we call "juvenile delinquency." This social aspect can easily be reconciled with the ultra-Romantic conception of the self that underlies the novel. Observers have pointed out the element of latter-day Romanticism in juvenile delinquency. In recent years, some novels and films dealing openly with this social phenomenon have borrowed features from *L'Etranger*, a work that, outwardly at least, has nothing to do with it. The hero of the film *A bout de souffle*, for instance, half voluntarily kills a policeman, thus becoming a "good criminal" after Meursault's fashion. The *theme* of juvenile delinquency is absent from *L'Etranger* because the novel is the literary equivalent of the action, its perfect *analogon*.

L'Etranger is certainly no accurate portrayal of the society in which it was created. Should we say, therefore, as the formalists do, that it is a "world of its own," that it is wholly independent from this society? The novel *reverses* the laws of our society but this reversal is not an absence of relationship. It is a more complex relationship that involves negative as well as positive factors and that cannot be expressed in the mechanical terms of the old realism or positivism. It is an indirect relationship that must be apprehended if we want to apprehend the esthetic structure itself. We have just seen that the only way to illuminate the esthetic structure of *L'Etranger* as an integrated structure is to resort to the social phenomenon called "juvenile delinquency." *L'Etranger* is not independent from the social reality it overturns, since this overturning is a social attitude among others and a very typical one. The autonomy of the structure may appear absolute to the writer at the time of his writing, and to the uncritical reader, but it is only relative. *L'Etranger* reflects the world view of the juvenile delinquent with unmatched perfection precisely because it is not aware of reflecting anything, except, of course, the innocence of its hero and the injustice of his judges.

Camus wrote *L'Etranger* against the "judges" or, in other words, against the middle class who are his sole potential readers. Instead of rejecting the book as the author had half hoped, half feared, these bourgeois readers showered it with praise. The "judges," obviously, did not recognize their portrait when they saw it. They, too, cursed the iniquitous judges and howled for clemency. They, too, identified with the innocent victim and they acclaimed Meursault as a Galahad of sunworshiping "authenticity." The public turned out, in short, to be made not of judges, as the author had mistakenly believed, but of generous lawyers like the author himself.

Since all the admirers of the early Camus share, to some extent, in the guilt of the "generous lawyer," they too should be present in *La Chute*. And they are, in the person of Clamence's silent listener. The man has nothing to say because Clamence answers *his* questions and objections almost before they are formulated in *our* minds. At the end of the book, this man confesses his identity; he, too, is a generous lawyer.

Thus, Clamence is addressing each one of us personally, leaning toward *me* across a narrow café table and looking straight in *my* eyes. His monologue is dotted with exclamations, interjections, and apostrophes; every three lines we have an "allons," "tiens," "quoi!," "eh bein!," "ne trouvez vous pas," "mon cher compatriote," etc. The style of *La Chute* is the exact antithesis of the impersonal and antirhetorical *écriture blanche*. Gone is the false detachment of Meursault. We have shifted from the "restrained indignation" of the generous lawyer, as Clamence aptly defines it, to the open theatricality of a self-confessed and yet insurmountable bad faith. The studiously cheap and cacophonic symbolism of *La Chute* is a parody of the serious symbolic works of the past.

As he questions the authenticity of *L'Etranger* and similar works, Camus questions the question itself. *La Chute*, no less than *L'Etranger*, is directed against all potential readers because it is directed against the lawyers in a world where only lawyers are left. The technique of spiritual aggression has become more subtle but its aim has not changed.

Why does Clamence point out to us that his new posture is still one of bad faith? He undermines his own position in order to prevent others from undermining it. After deriding the generous lawyer, he mockingly describes himself as a penitent-judge. Slyly anticipating his readers, whom he knows to be adept at gleaning moral comfort from the most sinister parables, he gives a new twist to the now familiar serpent, hoping to keep one step ahead of everybody else in a game of self-justification that has turned into a game of self-accusation.

Let the judge repudiate judgment and he becomes a judge in disguise, a lawyer; let the lawyer repudiate the disguise and he becomes a penitent-judge; let the penitent-judge. . . . We are spiraling down the circles of a particularly nasty hell, but this more and more precipitous *chute* is perhaps not so fatal as it seems. The penitent-judge does not believe in his role half as much as the generous lawyer did. The conclusion of *La Chute* is a final pirouette as well, perhaps, as the image of what may happen to a world entirely given over to the lawyers and the penitent-judges.

The universal need for self-justification haunts all modern trial literature. But there are different levels of awareness. The so called "myth" of the trial can be approached from several mutually exclusive perspectives. In *L'Etranger*, the real question is that of the innocence and guilt of the protagonists. The criminal is innocent and the judges are guilty. In the more conventional ego-nourishing fiction, the criminal is usually guilty and the judges innocent. But this difference is really secondary. In both cases, "good" and "bad" are rigid concepts; the verdict of the judges is challenged but not their vision.

La Chute goes higher and deeper. Clamence is still busy proving that he is "good" and that other people are "bad," but his systems of classification keep breaking down. The real question is no longer "who is innocent, who is guilty?" but "why do we, all of us, have to keep judging and being judged?" It is a more interesting question, the very question of Dostoevsky. In *La Chute*, Camus lifts trial literature back to the level of this great predecessor.

The first Camus did not realize how far-reaching, how pervasive the evil of judgment is. He felt that he was outside judgment because he condemned those who condemn. Using Gabriel Marcel's terminology, we may say Meursault viewed evil as something outside himself, a *problem* that concerned the judges alone, whereas Clamence knows that he himself is involved. Evil is the *mystery* of a pride that, as it condemns others, unwittingly condemns itself. It is the pride of Oedipus, another hero of trial literature, always uttering the curses that result in his own undoing. Reciprocity between the I and the Thou asserts itself in the very efforts I make to deny it: "The sentence which you pass against your fellow men," says Clamence, "is always flung back into your face where it effects quite a bit of damage."

The outsider is really inside, but he is not aware of it. This lack of awareness determines the esthetic as well as the spiritual limitations of *L'Etranger*. A man who feels the urge to write a trial novel is not really "in love with the sun." He does not belong to the sunny Mediterranean but to the fogs of Amsterdam.

The world in which we live is one of perpetual judgment. It must be our Judeo-Christian heritage, still active within us. We are not healthy pagans. We are not Jews, either, since we have no Law. But we are not real

Christians, since we keep judging. Who are we? A Christian cannot help feeling that the answer is close at hand: "thou art inexcusable, o man, whosoever thou art that judgest; for wherein thou judgest another, thou condemnest thyself; for thou that judgest dost the same things." Did Camus realize that all the themes of *La Chute* are in Paul's *Epistles?* If he had, would he have drawn from the analogy, and from the answers of Paul, the conclusions that a Christian would draw? Nobody can answer these questions.

Meursault was guilty of judgment but he never found out; Clamence alone found out. The two heroes may be viewed as a single one whose career describes a single itinerary somewhat analogous to the itinerary of the great Dostoevskian heroes. Like Raskolnikov, like Dmitri Karamazov, Meursault-Clamence first pictured himself as the victim of a judicial error, but he finally realized that the sentence was just, even if the judges were personally unjust, because the Self can provide only a grotesque parody of Justice.

The universal dimension of *La Chute* can be reached only through its most personal, almost intimate dimension. The two are really one; the structure of the work is one and its significance is one. Openly, at least, this significance is entirely negative. But the positive aspects are summed up in one sentence of the Nobel Prize acceptance speech. Camus opposes, in their order, his two fundamental attitudes, as a creator and as a man, leaving no doubt as to the personal significance of Clamence's confession:

> L'art . . . oblige . . . l'artiste à ne pas s'isoler; il le soumet à la vérité la plus humble et la plus universelle. Et celui qui, souvent, a choisi son destin d'artiste parce qu'il se sentait différent, apprend bien vite qu'il ne nourrira son art, et sa différence, qu'en avouant sa ressemblance avec tous.

WILLIAM M. MANLY

Journey to Consciousness:
The Symbolic Pattern of Camus's L'Etranger

Although a good deal has been written about *L'Etranger* in the light of Camus's philosophic insights in *Le Mythe de Sisyphe*, the verbal similarities between these two works have been used only sporadically in interpreting the novel. Carl Viggiani, whose essay on *L'Etranger* appears to have dealt most fully with the symbolic undercurrent of the novel and Meursault's relation to Sisyphus, has concentrated almost solely on detached archetypal motifs while largely neglecting any sort of progressive or "novelistic" development of the protagonist as he moves from his mother's funeral to his final jail cell. I propose to demonstrate such a consistent development by viewing Meursault's adventure as a parable of mental awakening or coming to consciousness which corresponds in detailed thematic and imagistic ways to the adventure of the mind in *Le Mythe de Sisyphe*.

Le Mythe, published less than a year after *L'Etranger*, contains Camus's impassioned search for a philosophic position which could clearly and steadily confront the inescapable facts of human isolation and mortality while yet remaining creative. He claimed the work was not designed to reveal a "philosophie absurde" but a "sensibilité absurde," an intention which is readily apparent in its poetic style and emotional tone. Camus's earlier work, *L'Etranger*, is quite as clearly concerned with man's consciousness in the face of ultimate realities. The novel is constructed around Meursault's three

From *PMLA* 79, no. 3 (June 1964). © 1964 *PMLA*.

confrontations of death: his mother's death at the beginning of the tale, the Arab's death in the middle, and the prospect of his own death at the end. All three of these confrontations contribute to Meursault's growing consciousness of the sheer impersonality and human negation implied in death, and all three confrontations he attempts in one way or another to elude, but ultimately fails to do so.

Meursault's calm indifference to his mother's death in the opening scenes (he significantly feels more involved with his mother at the novel's conclusion) subtly gives rise to what Sartre terms a "sense of shock"; to the extent that death and grief are realities which do not touch this protagonist, his perfunctory behavior appears to reveal a deeper disengagement from reality than the word "unconventional" implies. Although the novel's personal point of view invites sympathy with Meursault, it is precisely the quality of sympathetic awareness that seems lacking in his attitude toward his mother, Marie, Céleste, Raymond, and his life in general in the first section; it is an attitude which is not as much "sincere" or "unhypocritical" as it is simply uninvolved. In the light of Camus's preoccupation with different states of consciousness in Le Mythe, it is suggested that Meursault's early behavior falls into a symbolic pattern which is characteristic of the novel as a whole.

Camus writes that the man who is unaware of the absurd condition lives a life of habitual day-to-day actions in a routine that smothers thought: "Lever, tramway, quatre heures de bureau ou d'usine, repas, tramway, quatre heures de travail, repas, sommeil et lundi mardi mercredi jeudi vendredi et samedi sur le même rhythme, cette route se suit aisément la plupart du temps." Meursault, it will be noted, shows similarities to this man of habit (he is disturbed and apologetic about the break in clerical routine that his mother's funeral causes, and he is not attracted to the suggestion that he take a job in Paris), which in turn intimates that his indifference toward the funeral may be of richer import than the casual eye might suspect. It symbolically suggests a failure to face with full consciousness the implications of death itself, the first duty of the absurd man.

In these terms the descriptive details of the funeral proceedings take on a hitherto unremarked importance. The continual insistence on "whiteness" and "light" in the mortuary, for example, where Meursault maintains his sleepy vigil, takes on a special resonance when viewed in association with metaphors of intense consciousness in Le Mythe. The mortuary is "une salle très claire, blanchie à la chaux et recouverte d'une verrière"; within the room is an Arab woman with a "sarrau blanc," a doorkeeper with a "moustache blanche," and a sick woman with a white bandage about her face: "On ne voyait que la blancheur du bandeau dans son visage." The effect of light on all this whiteness is to make the "petite morgue" into a place which reverberates painfully against Meursault's eyes. When the doorkeeper puts on the lights, he remarks "j'ai été aveuglé par l'éclaboussement soudain de la lumière," and later asks that one of the lights be extinguished. The doorkeeper tells him it is not possible.

In the face of this stark reality, Meursault's impulse is to doze as he feels constantly fatigued in this room of death. Yet even as he tries to shut out the situation he is being made uneasy. A group of figures enters: "C'est un frôlement qui m'a réveillé. D'avoir fermé les yeux, la pièce m'a paru encore plus éclatante de blancheur. Devant moi, il n'y avait pas une ombre et chaque objet, chaque angle, toutes les courbes se dessinaient avec une pureté blessante pour les yeux. C'est à ce moment que les amis de maman sont entrés. Ils étaient en tout une dizaine, et ils glissaient en silence dans cette lumière aveuglante. . . . Je les voyais comme je n'ai jamais vu personne et pas un détail de leurs visages ou de leurs habits ne m'échappait. Pourtant je ne les entendais pas et j'avais peine à croire à leur réalité."

An insistent, repetitive emphasis on eyes and sight is noticeable in the above passage: "D'avoir fermé les yeux"; "une pureté blessante pour les yeux"; "Je les voyais comme je n'ai jamais vu personne"; and this emphasis is constantly in association with "lumière." Such a concentration on eyes, sight, and light suggests a passage from *Le Mythe* which associates these images with awakening consciousness: "'La prière,' dit Alain, 'c'est quand la nuit vient sur la pensée.' 'Mais il faut que l'esprit rencontre la nuit,' répondent les mystiques les et existentiels. Certes, mais non pas cette nuit qui naît sous les yeux fermés et par la seule volonté de l'homme—nuit sombre et close que l'esprit suscite pour s'y perdre. S'il doit rencontrer une nuit, que ce soit plutôt celle du désespoir qui reste lucide, *nuit polaire, veille de l'esprit, d'où se lèvera peut-être cette clarté blanche et intacte qui dessine chaque objet dans la lumière de l'intelligence*" (my italics).

The "nuit" which has descended over the mortuary is not being met by Meursault, whose "vigil" (the same word "veille" is used in both works) resembles not the lucid encounter of the conscious intellect but the "yeux fermés" of comfortable thinkers. Striking similarities exist between Camus's vigil of consciousness in *Le Mythe* and Meursault's vigil of death in the mortuary. Each object in both is "dessiné"—outlined—by the light, and the light in both is a brilliant whiteness. Camus describes the life without absurd consciousness in *Le Mythe* as "une vie sans éclat," a metaphor which further suggests that Meursault's weariness in the face of light may be metaphysically dramatic. Taken together, the above associations imply that Meursault's failure to waken physically to his situation is symbolically associated with a more metaphysical failure to become aware of death's profound implications.

The failure is not absolute, however. Meursault's uneasiness and discomfort seem to hint that he is troubled, at odd moments, by a deeper sense of his situation. The old people who surround the body are first dismissed as "unreal," but later he remarks, "J'ai eu un moment l'impression ridicule qu'ils étaient là pour me juger." The same disturbed feeling is aroused by the old man who stares fixedly at him while he dozes, "comme s'il n'attendait que mon réveil." The dreamlike starkness of the mortuary forces every detail into sharp relief and seems to charge the word "réveil" with more than literal meaning. The old people who are in attendance are awake in a significant sense because they are closer to death than is Meursault and feel it as a conditioning factor in their lives. This curious "wakefulness" is what separates them from the ordinary world of "café" and "bavardage" which occupy the doorkeeper and Meursault and is perhaps the underlying reason why the doorkeeper recognizes no community with them (they are always spoken of as "ils," "les autres," or "les vieux"). Yet a glimmer of insight into the importance of death for a man's life is afforded to Meursault as he appears to reflect on the wake: "J'avais même l'impression que cette morte, couchée au milieu d'eux, ne signifiait rien à leurs yeux. Mais je crois maintenant que c'etait une impression fausse." The "maintenant" of this passage introduces into the account a time later than the opening "aujourd'hui" and would appear to suggest a Meursault who is at the point of death himself in the final scenes of the novel. From such a perspective he would see with new eyes the implications of "cette morte" to the living watchers.

He obtains a further insight into the unblinkable reality of death and the absurd as he follows his mother's coffin in the merciless sun the following day. The glare which makes him dizzy seems to transform the landscape into something "inhumain et déprimant"; he feels the sun to be as brutal and inescapable as was the light in the mortuary. The nurse at the procession tells him, "'Si on va doucement, on risque une insolation. Mais si on va trop vite, on est en transpiration et dans l'église on attrape un chaud et froid.' Elle avait raison. Il n'y avait pas d'issue." The harsh sense of alienation from nature which Meursault's imagery conveys throughout the sun-drenched funeral procession, his perception of something "inhuman" in the landscape, invites attention to a passage in *Le Mythe* where Camus describes a stage in absurd awareness: "Un degré plus bas et voici l'étrangeté: s'apercevoir que le monde est 'épais,' entrevoir á quel point une pierre est étrangère, nous est irréductible, *avec quelle intensité la nature, un paysage peut nous nier. Au fond de toute beauté gît quelque chose d'inhumain*" (my italics).

Meursault has glimpsed the foreignness and inhumanity of a world which negates man's hopes and rationality. He has seen, fitfully, at moments of crisis, that one cannot elude such a world ("Il n'y avait pas d'issue"), but his perceptions have no consequences for him because they do not become the center of a conscious encounter with this world—the true role of the absurd hero. His general metaphysical condition in this first section may be likened to that of the Algerians in Camus's short piece, "L'Eté à Alger" of whom the author writes: "[Ce peuple] a mis tous ses biens sur cette terre et reste dès lors sans défense contre la mort" (*Noces*).

It has been generally observed that Camus's recurring imagery of sea and sun is derived in large measure from a boyhood spent on the North African littoral, and that his retrospective nostalgia for the barbaric, physical world of the Algerians is reflected throughout his personal essays and novels. Yet it is worth noting that Camus's rapport with the deeply sensual world of the Algerians is always conditioned by the knowledge that their honesty in confronting realities is to a large extent unconscious, and that their potential for greatness is to a large extent unrealized. Awareness of one's condition is vital to the absurd wager and the true absurd hero; in this respect the Algerians remain a "peuple enfant." The Meursault we meet in part I of *L'Etranger* is a member of this unengaged and metaphysically unaware community of Algerians Camus had known as a boy. His life, like the lives Camus describes in *Noces*, is wholly cast in the present. Meursault in prison remarks of his earlier life: "J'étais toujours pris par ce qui allait arriver, par aujourd'hui ou par demain." His attitude toward death, also, has affinities with the Algerian attitude. Camus writes in *Noces*, "Tout ce qui touche à la mort est ici ridicule ou odieux," and a bit further on he adds, "Comment faire comprendre pourtant que ces images de la mort ne se séparent jamais de la vie?" In *L'Etranger* it is evident that images of death and life are not wholly separated in Meursault's mind at his mother's funeral; his tendency is to see death in terms of physical details which do not require an order of thought distinct from his present routine.

The "Algerian" quality of Meursault's consciousness is maintained until the encounter with the Arab on the beach which ends the first section and begins the process of moulding him into an absurd protagonist. In this second confrontation of death, at which Meursault is no longer passive but active, the presence of sun and heat again show a certain verbal similarity with the language of awakening consciousness in *Le Mythe de Sisyphe*. *Le Mythe* is not strictly a philosophic work which employs a tightly restricted, logical vocabulary; rather it is written as an adventure of the mind, and the language used to describe this quest is often novelistic. Metaphors of climate and landscape are frequently used to convey mental states: "paysages spirituels"; "ces lieux déserts et sans eaux où la pensée arrive à ses confins"; "je veux savoir auparavant si la pensée peut vivre dans ces déserts"; or the longer phrase: "On sent bien qu'il y a un climat commun aux esprits que l'on vient de rappeler. Dire que ce climat est meurtrier, c'est à peine jouer sur les mots. Vivre sous ce ciel étouffant commande qu'on en sorte ou qu'on y reste." This emphasis on deserts without water and oppressive skies calls attention to Camus's characteristic way of conceiving mental experience and suggests the ground on which absurd awareness might begin.

Meursault was on such a ground of oppressive heat and light at his mother's funeral, and he encounters this metaphorical landscape of the mind again on the beach outside Algiers. As at the funeral procession, the sun beats down on him with an insistent, disruptive force: "C'était le même soleil que le jour où j'avais enterré maman et, comme alors, le front surtout me faisait mal et toutes ses veines battaient ensemble sous la peau." Once again Meursault attempts to elude the stark pressure of light and heat that threatens to unseat his mind: "Je pensais à la source fraîche derrière le rocher. J'avais envie de retrouver le murmure de son eau, *envie de fuir le soleil, l'effort, et les pleurs de femme, envie enfin de retrouver l'ombre et son repos*" (my italics). The phrase "les pleurs de femme" brings together Marie, the mourners at his mother's funeral, and the cries of Raymond's mistress—all of whom represent involvements he has avoided. The word "repos" and his desire for shade recall his weariness in the face of light and sun in the mortuary and at the funeral.

The Arab he encounters appears to lose human integrity and to be allied with the impersonal reality of the sunswept beach in wielding a knife which probes Meursault's eyes with light. Carl Viggiani writes of this confrontation: "Camus's use of the sun as the symbol of the ultimate vision of truth in "L'Eté" makes it probable that here too the sun, with its terrible brilliance, is what lights the central truth, that is, death." From a similar viewpoint, S. Beynon John finds the sun in the beach scene and at the funeral to be symbolic of "violence and destruction." This essay would suggest that these insights be taken a step further: it would appear that not only the sun, but (as the white glare of the mortuary suggests) "lumière" in general is employed by Camus in a recurrent pattern which in moments of crisis is highly symbolic. Furthermore, the metaphorical use of light in *Le Mythe* strongly suggests that the "violence" of this pattern is associated with what Camus conceives to be the mental shock of dawning absurd awareness, and that the association of this pattern with death is designed to dramatize the metaphysical ground of that awakening. Camus's recurring emphasis on a heat and glare that disturb Meursault's normal processes of thought, together with his repeated stress on "le front," the symbolic source of consciousness— these suggest that the pressure in the beach scene is toward a delirium which will destroy the mental poise Meursault has maintained by staying uninvolved. A sense of the world's potential for negation rises to meet him as it meets every man who takes thought.

The suggestion that a symbolic waking to consciousness is at issue in this crucial beach scene is reinforced by the descriptive details of the actual shooting. Unsettled by the sun and not fully in control, Meursault shoots the Arab five times. In this moment he realizes that something basic and irrevocable has happened to his life: "La gâchette a cédé, j'ai touché le ventre poli de la crosse et c'est là, dans le bruit à la fois sec et assourdissant, que tout a commencé. J'ai secoué la sueur et le soleil. J'ai compris que j'avais détruit l'équilibre du jour, le silence exceptionnel d'une plage où j'avias été heureux." Meursault's curious phrase, "détruit l'équilibre du jour," and the implication that he has shattered the calm surface of a life in which he had been happy, invite attention to the following passage from *Le Mythe de Sisyphe*: "Tant que l'esprit se tait dans le monde immobile de ses espoirs, tout se reflète et s'ordonne dans l'unité de sa nostalgie. Mais à son premier mouvement, ce monde se fêle et s'écroule: une infinité d'éclats miroitants s'offrent à la connaissance. Il faut désespérer d'en reconstruire jamais la surface familière et tranquille qui nous donnerait la paix du cœur." In view of the symbolic and metaphorical associations that exist between light and consciousness in *Le Mythe*, and the stress on the penetrating quality of light on the beach in *L'Etranger*, the shattering effect Meursault feels after the shooting may be fruitfully viewed as having a relation to the "premier mouvement" of his mind. This "premier mouvement" is the beginning of absurd awareness, which is described in *Le Mythe* as a mental fragmentation leading to a destruction of mental equilibrium—precisely the sensations that Meursault feels after killing the Arab.

In the light of these associations, his emphasis on this moment as a beginning is important. The expression "tout a commencé" is used directly after he shoots the Arab and is used again in prison to indicate a hopeless reality which must be faced: "En réalité, je n'étais pas réellement en prison les premiers jours. . . . C'est seulement après la première et la seule visite de Marie que tout a commencé." Emphasis on absurd consciousness as a "beginning" also occurs in *Le Mythe*: "Un jour seulement, le 'pourquoi' s'élève et tout commence dans cette lassitude teintée d'étonnement. 'Commence,' ceci est important. La lassitude est à la fin des actes d'une vie machinale, *mais elle inaugure en même temps le mouvement de la conscience. Elle l'éveille et elle provoque la suite*" (my italics).

Camus defines the "sentiment de l'absurdité" as "cet incalculable sentiment qui prive l'esprit du sommeil nécessaire à sa vie" (*Mythe*). In prison Meursault is to hear an ice cream vendor and think: "Oui, c'était l'heure où, il y avait bien longtemps, je me sentais content. Ce qui m'attendait alors, c'était toujours un sommeil léger et sans rêves." His shots on the beach have destroyed forever the possibility of easy, dreamless sleep. On the basis of associations which connect sleep and lassitude with a lack of mental perceptivity or with self-deception, it is suggested that Meursault's encounter with the Arab marks the opening stage in a now conscious confrontation of irrationality and hostility.

Section II of *L'Etranger* dramatizes the slow transformation of a once insouciant, comfortable mind into the lucid, open-eyed, absurd hero who emerges in the final pages. This full transformation is brought about by the final crisis in Meursault's symbolic journey: his third experience with the fact and idea of death which he has tried to hold from him without success. An awareness of death, which Camus finds in *Le Mythe* to give life meaning, begins at last to operate meaningfully on the protagonist of *L'Etranger*. He now begins to feel what the watchful old people in the mortuary felt while he dozed: the intensity imparted to life by one's own imminent death.

During his first days in prison, Meursault hopes vaguely for something to happen ("J'attendais vaguement quelque événement nouveau"), but gradually he realizes that hope is not justified: "j'ai senti que j'étais chez moi dans ma cellule et que ma vie s'y arrêtait." Camus observes in *Le Mythe* that the cessation of hope is a necessary preliminary to a full awareness of the absurd condition. "Eluder, voilà le jeu constant," he writes. "L'élision type, l'élision mortelle qui fait le troisième thème de cet essai, c'est l'espoir."

But it is only after Meursault has been convicted and sentenced to death that the true dialogue between the "silence déraisonnable du monde" and his need for meaning begins. One of the early signs of this encounter is his obsessive desire to find a loophole in the law's seemingly irresistible machinery. The desire to find "a way out" of the prison of finitude is one of the first mental steps that the truly aware man takes to reach the desert of the absurd position. "Ce qui m'intéresse en ce moment," Meursault remarks in his cell, "c'est d'échapper à la mécanique, de savoir si l'inévitable peut avoir une issue." The abstract quality of this statement (consider "d'échapper à la mécanique" and the substantive use of "inévitable," language which seems much too philosophical for the earlier Meursault to whom everything is "égal") begins to suggest the quality of thought in *Le Mythe de Sisyphe*. Meursault's reasoning grows steadily more rigorous as he becomes conscious of his position: "Malgré ma bonne volonté, je ne pouvais pas accepter cette certitude insolente. Car enfin, il y avait une disproportion ridicule entre le jugement qui l'aviait fondée et son déroulement imperturbable à partir du moment où ce jugement avait été prononcé."

In a passage from *Le Mythe* Camus characterizes the principle of the absurd with the example of a man charging a machine gun. The act is absurd, he writes, "en vertu de la disproportion qui existe entre son intention et la réalité qui l'attend, de la contradiction que je puis saisir entre ses forces réelles et le but qui'il se propose." The disproportion that Meursault perceives between the vague and irrational judgment of the court and the enormous gravity of that judgment's consequences, is precisely the sense of "disproportion" which Camus feels to be inherent in the human condition when properly faced. So too, behind Meursault's musings on death's "certitude insolente" is an echo of Camus's remarks on the inevitability of death in *Le Mythe*. "L'horreur vient en réalité du côté mathématique de l'événement," he writes. "Ce côté élémentaire et définitif de l'aventure fait le contenu du sentiment absurde."

The "sentiment absurde" is thus gradually achieved by Meursault's burgeoning awareness of how his coming death, faced as an inescapable negation of his life, brings him a new sense of self that he had never previously grasped. His transformation into the absurd hero at the close of his symbolic journey is most clearly dramatized during his interview with the prison chaplain. Meursault's dialogue with this arch-eluder reveals a number of major characteristics of the absurd reasoner which are to be found in the following passage of *Le Mythe*: "On lui assure que c'est péché d'orgueil [to persist in absurdist reasoning], mais il n'entend pas la notion de péché; que peut-être l'enfer est au bout, mais il n'a pas assez d'imagination pour se représenter cet étrange avenir; qu'il perd la vie immortelle, mais cela lui paraît futile. On voudrait lui faire reconnaître sa culpabilité. Lui se sent innocent. A vrai dire, il ne sent que cela, son innocence irréparable. C'est elle qui lui permet tout. Ainsi ce qu'il exige de lui-même, c'est de vivre *seulement* avec ce qu'il sait, de s'arranger de ce qui est et ne rien faire intervenir qui ne soit certain. On lui répond que rien ne l'est. Mais ceci du moins est une certitude. C'est avec elle qu'il a affaire: il veut savoir s'il est possible de vivre sans appel."

This passage clearly suggests the metaphysical grounds of Meursault's dissatisfaction with the chaplain. The phrase "il n'entend pas la notion de péché," for example, is well illustrated by Meursault's remark: "Selon lui [the chaplain], la justice des hommes n'était rien et la justice de Dieu tout. J'ai remarqué que c'était la première qui m'avait condamné. Il m'a répondu qu'elle n'avait pas, pour autant, lavé mon péché. *Je lui ai dit que je ne savais pas ce qu'était un péché*" (my italics).

Camus's phrase in *Le Mythe*, "On lui assure . . . qu'il perd la vie immortelle, mais cela lui paraît futile," is paralleled in *L'Etranger* by the following dialogue begun by the chaplain: "'Non, je ne peux pas vous croire. Je suis sûr qu'il vous est arrivé de souhaiter une autre vie.' Je lui ai répondu que naturellement, mais cela n'avait pas plus d'importance que de souhaiter d'être riche, de nager très vite ou d'avoir une bouche mieux faite. C'était du même ordre."

The statement from *Le Mythe*, "On voudrait lui faire reconnâitre sa culpabilité. Lui se sent innocent," is dramatized by Meursault's attitude before the magistrate who tells him, "Les criminels qui sont venus devant moi ont toujours pleuré devant cette image de la douleur"—at which Meursault thinks, "J'allais répondre que c'était justement parce qu'il s'agissait de criminels. Mais j'ai pensé que moi aussi j'étais comme eux. *C'était une idée à quoi je ne pouvais pas me faire*" (my italics).

The interview with the chaplain is brought to a violent close by Meursault's lucid rage against the falseness of hope and comfortable thinking: "Je me suis mis à crier à plein gosier et je l'ai insulté et je lui ai dit de ne pas prier, et qu'il valait mieux brûler que disparaître. . . . Il avait l'air si certain, n'est-ce pas? Pourtant, aucune de ses certitudes ne valait un cheveu de femme. Il n'était même pas sûr d'être en vie puisqu'il vivait comme un mort. Moi, j'avias l'air d'avoir les mains vides. Mais j'étais sûr de moi, sûr de tout, plus sûr que lui, sûr de ma vie et de cette mort qui allait venir." This argument clearly reveals an aroused Meursault who, in the face of his own death, is brought to a realization of truths which he had only dimly perceived earlier. He has been metamorphosed into an absurd reasoner who maintains his sovereignty of self-knowledge despite the solicitations of conventional escapes from the self. Having started as a shrinker from consciousness in section I, Meursault now has an awareness only slightly less rigorous in expression than the mentality exhibited in *Le Mythe de Sisyphe*—he has taken up the wager of the absurd.

Meursault has strong affinities with Camus's conception of Sisyphus in the closing description of him in his prison cell. Camus says of Sisyphus at the base of his mountain: "Chacun des grains de cette pierre, chaque éclat minéral de cette montagne pleine de nuit, à lui seule, forme un monde. La lutte elle-même vers les sommets suffit à remplir un cœur d'homme. Il faut imaginer Sisyphe heureux." So too, Meursault in his cell awaiting death feels the sounds and smells of the countryside to form "un monde" as they become intensified in memory by his predicament. He thinks back again to his mother and now understands why she too chose to struggle in the face of death's negation and took a "fiancé." Finally he thinks: "Et moi aussi, je me suis senti prêt à tout revivre. Comme si cette grande colère m'avait purgé du mal, vidé d'espoir, devant cette nuit chargée de signes et d'étoiles, je m'ouvrais pour la première fois à la tendre indifférence du monde. De l'éprouver si pareil à moi, si fraternel enfin, *j'ai senti que j'avais été heureux, et que je l'étais éncore*" (my italics).

A sense of the world's fraternal indifference has at last brought Meursault to a realization that he is, in fact, "coupable" as he vaguely felt himself to be in the early courtroom scenes. But from this perspective he sees that he is guilty not of simply breaking the laws of men, but guilty of the broader offense in which all men to some degree participate: he has become a part of an absurd universe. It is this universe which drove him to the violence against the unoffending Arab on the beach and it was the shooting which revealed to him his inescapable complicity in a world which negates human life.

This insight, it would seem, is Meursault's final step in his journey to consciousness; it is a step wherein he transcends his own ego and becomes one with that knowledge which has moved beneath his indifference throughout the early scenes of the novel. Abjuring the soft promises of the chaplain, who would give him hope in exchange for an integrity of conscious suffering ("il valait mieux brûler que disparaître"), Meursault chooses execration. "Pour que tout soit consommé, pour que je me sente moins seul, il me restait à souhaiter qu'il y ait beaucoup de spectateurs le jour de mon exécution et qu'ils m'accueillent avec des cris de haine." This strange desire for "cris de haine" is linked philosophically to his mother's desire to take a "fiancé" in old age; both ideas appear absurd and futile, yet Meursault sees that the very friction of one's resistance tö death asserts an inalienable core of identity. From an attempt to elude the implications of his fate at the hands of an irrational community, Meursault has, at the last, chosen to define himself by that fate. He has become like Sisyphus in the final chapters of *Le Mythe*: a being execrated by the gods yet one who knows himself fully only when face to face with the objects of that hatred—the solidity of his rock and the steepness of his mountain. Meursault has also become vaguely associated with Christ in this imagined scene of reviled execution. But the suggestion of Christ's crucifixion in Meursault's hoped for "consummation" is clearly an identification with Christ the sufferer not Christ the redeemer. Only on a cross of hatred can Meursault completely fulfill himself.

Meursault's slow coming to knowledge has at last ended with the paradox which *Le Mythe de Sisyphe* propounded more philosophically: Man, as part of an absurd existence, is least alienated from the sensation of being when he is most sensitive to that inhuman hostility that lurks beneath the mask of habit. To strip the mask is to feel to the last agony that grandeur in loneliness of Christ and Sisyphus.

A. D. NUTTALL

Did Meursault Mean to Kill the Arab?—
The Intentional Fallacy Fallacy

This essay is an attempt to resolve a complex and sophisticated question: is the artist's intention relevant to a critical appraisal of his work?—by answering what is, at first sight at least, a much simpler question: did Meursault, in Camus' *L'Etranger*, mean to kill the Arab? W. K. Wimsatt Jr. and Monroe C. Beardsley published in 1946 a singularly difficult and tortuous essay on the first of these questions. It is called 'The Intentional Fallacy' and has become famous; indeed the phrase 'intentional fallacy' has passed into the language and found a warm welcome even before its meaning has become clear, and one could hardly ask for greater fame than *that*. In the same year the first English translation of Camus' *L'Etranger* appeared. Perhaps more than one university lecturer, wearied by the theoretic involutions of Wimsatt and Beardsley, turned for solace to the latest novel and found instead of solace the red sand and pitiless sun, the stark mortality of Meursault's world. Such a reader would have the experience of passing from evident complexity to enigmatic simplicity; of moving from an abstract disquisition on the relation between intention and public performance to a scrupulously observed concrete instance; instead of the intricate cogitations of Wimsatt and Beardsley, an implied question, itself more radical than any they had thought to ask: what is an 'intentional' action?

From *Critical Quarterly* 10 (1968). © 1968 by *Critical Quarterly*.

II

A great part of the difficulty of the essay 'The Intentional Fallacy' springs naturally from the intrinsic complexity of the subject. It is, however, consistent with this view to suspect that a certain amount of our difficulty may be traced to a less respectable source, that is to confusions in the thought of the essay itself. Many of these have already been publicly discussed, perhaps most effectively in Mr. Frank Cioffi's admirable article. I wish here to isolate just one of them.

Wimsatt and Beardsley seem to oscillate between two essentially opposed views. The first is relatively straightforward and, in my opinion, erroneous. It is this: the critical reading of a poem and the acquisition of 'background information' have nothing to do with each other; judgments formed in criticism are, in principle, not modifiable by arguments drawn from 'background information'. Thus the authors cite with approval Matthiessen's contention that T. S. Eliot's contrasting of the modern Thames with the Elizabethan river requires no reading of Spenser for its proper appreciation, although (as a matter of merely historical interest) Spenser's line, 'Sweet Thames, run softly till I end my song' is actually quoted in Eliot's poem. The notion here seems to be that although poems may be constructed, like mosaics, from fragments of other authors, to point out this fact is to say something about the psychological genesis of the poem, certainly, but nothing material to a critical reading. If an objector were to say, 'Do you hold to this view even if it could shown that Eliot was writing with a clear awareness of the context, in the original author, of his quotation?' Wimsatt and Beardsley might well reply, 'When you say Eliot has this awareness, are you merely describing Eliot's state of mind at the time of writing? If so, our answer must be that this is of purely psychological interest. If, on the other hand, you mean that Eliot's awareness shows in his writing, then of course it is of interest to us as critics; but then, if it shows, it shows; there is no need for Dryasdust to point it out.' It is not hard to expose the sophistry of this possible reply: it is often impossible to tell whether an awareness of context is shown or not without first obtaining information about the original passage. There need, of course, be no question here of investigating Eliot's state of mind at the time of writing. All that is necessary is that certain turns of phrase, certain echoes will click into place with a coherency which suggests a complex relationship between archetype and ectype. Such echoes and correspondences could not have been perceived at all by a reader entirely ignorant of the original. Moreover, to cite a single instance in which (to grant for the moment Matthiessen's contention) the background information is of no critical value is scarcely the most effective way to convince a sceptic.

Wimsatt and Beardsley have, in effect, put the following case: 'Background information cannot, in principle, have any effect on our critical judgments, and to show that this is so we offer a line where it has none.' Plainly, an ordinary confirming instance carries no cogency in such a situation; what is rather needed is an *invidious* instance, which can yet be made to yield the required lesson. Wimsatt and Beardsley ought to be saying '. . . to show that this is so we offer a line where everyone has always assumed that the background information is critically relevant but where we can demonstrate that, essentially, it is not'. But this Wimsatt and Beardsley cannot do; not because of the insufficient reading or weak memory, but because no-one can; because it is impossible.

III

Certainly there is a difference for most people between reading *The Waste Land* before, and after reading a commentary (I have in mind here, not Eliot's notes, but the sort of commentary provided in the Norton Anthology of English Literature). Now if we hold that the first reading, *sans* commentary, is the right one, what are we to say to a man who, by some strange chance, happens to have read the Sanskrit *Upanishads*, *From Ritual to Romance*, and *The Golden Bough*? Does his knowledge *unfit* him for reading the poem?

Perhaps we should limit ourselves for the moment to speaking, not of the right and the wrong reading, but of better and worse readings.

But Wimsatt and Beardsley do not commit themselves to the view I have just attacked. Instead, as I have said, they oscillate. After commending Matthiessen, they note: 'Eliot's allusions work when we know them—and to a great extent even when we do not know them, through their suggestive power.' The phrasing of this suggests scholarly caution, but what is really happening here? That qualifying 'to a great extent' in fact gives away the whole principle. If it is only in the majority of cases that background information has no critical relevance, there must remain a minority of cases when it *has*. Obviously no conscientious critic could afford to neglect the commentaries and background information as long as that were true. An apparently radical—even revolutionary—thesis has shrunk to a platitude: that historical information is often dry and unexciting, but occasionally it can illuminate a line of verse.

Our authors seek to remedy this unhappy situation by means of an epigrammatic distinction. We must separate, they say, evidence relating to the meaning of words (ironically enough called internal evidence) from

evidence concerning the biography of the poet, the circumstances of composition, *etc.* (ironically enough—for it all derives from private or idiosyncratic
sources—called external evidence). They also admit the possibility of a third
kind, to which I shall turn in a moment. Of the two kinds so far described the
first is critically useful while the second is not. This is a neat distinction, but
very vulnerable. The authors have achieved their paradox only by blurring
the normal distinction between internal and external evidence. 'Internal
evidence' means simply 'evidence provided in the work'. The solemn-secre-
tive tone of Donne's 'A Valediction: Forbidding Mourning' is internal
evidence for the dating of that poem; Walton's *Life* is external. The reference
in Act IV of *Macbeth* to the union of the Kingdoms is internal evidence for
the date of that play; Dr. Simon Forman's description of the performance he
saw is external. Glossarial information about the meaning of words in a poem
normally utilizes external evidence—that is, it collates other uses of the same
word from other writers. The evidence used in determining the meaning of
words in our older literature is usually external.

Secondly, it looks as if this distinction will not in any case do the work
for which it was designed. Even the biographer cannot safely be ignored by
the critic. Certainly I am willing to grant at once that biographical work done
on, say, Shakespeare has contributed very little to our critical understanding
of that poet. The contribution to criticism made by the immense work of E.
K. Chambers is grotesquely small; grotesque, that is, in comparison with the
richness of the scholarship employed. Theories about the Dark Lady of the
Sonnets have been critically barren. But (and this is the point) we cannot be
confident that they will always be barren. Oscar Wilde's theory that Mr. W.
H. was an actor called Willie Hughes who played the part of Rosalind in *As
You Like It* would certainly, if it were established, modify our reading of the
Sonnets. The imagery of shadows and glasses, in particular, would be
enriched by the presence of an unsuspected theme—the relation between the
creator and the interpreter of a drama, the maker and the mask, the magician
and his creature, poet and player. The sonnet beginning 'What is your
substance whereof you are made' *feels* different to a man who has just read
Wilde's essay. Similarly, Leslie Hotson's conjecture about the identity and
history of Shakespeare's 'Mr. W. H.' could, if true, alter the whole character
of Sonnet 125—alter, and in this case diminish. But these are weak examples,
partly because their historical support is weak. Let us take one which is
strong and clear. Can any reader doubt that Milton's line 'O dark, dark, dark,
amid the blaze of noon' carries a special power because it is the utterance
either of a blind poet or of one shortly to become so? The fact that this is a
commonplace piece of information is beside the point. It is largely because
of the work of historians that it is commonplace. What, in these circum-

stances, is the conscientious anti-intentionalist to do? Repress his human reaction to the poet he knows? Endeavour to forget Milton's blindness? Restrict himself to the pure reading? But why should we, any more, believe in the pure reading? Such literary asceticism has nothing to commend it. Indeed, it can lead, I am sure, to mortification of the sensibility.

IV

But perhaps I have been too hasty. It could be argued that all my objections were anticipated by Wimsatt and Beardsley when they provided that third category of evidence, the category I omitted to describe. Under this heading falls all evidence of a private or semiprivate nature which can clarify special meanings given to a word, either by an individual author, or by a coterie of which he is a member. The critical relevance of this sort of evidence is readily admitted by Wimsatt and Beardsley on the ground that it teaches us not just the intention of the author (which *is* irrelevant) but also the meaning of the words. The crucial criterion here, however, seems at first sight to be semantic: that biographical information which makes no contribution to philology, to our knowledge of word-meanings, is without critical relevance. But in none of the cases I cited is our knowledge of the *meaning* of the words modified, in the ordinary dictionary sense of that term. Milton did not use the word 'dark' in a special, private *sense* because of his blindness. Thus, if the criterion is interpreted strictly, the theories of Wilde and Hotson and the biographical information about Milton do not satisfy it. The evident fact that these several considerations do affect our critical interpretation then becomes an embarrassment to Wimsatt and Beardsley, which their provision of a third category has failed to scotch. If on the other hand we relax our terminology and allow 'meaning' to cover impact, resonance, effect and the like, then all my examples might well be admitted to the status of critical relevance. But at what cost? It seems that we have been diverted once again with the now familiar party-trick of the disappearing thesis. We are left with the proposition that biographical information is not critically relevant unless it affects our critical judgement—a disguised tautology from which few will trouble to withhold their assent.

Of course biography and literary criticism are two different things. The biographer wants to know who (in fact) was X, where (in fact) did he do what he did. The critic usually wants to know: what is the precise tenor of this passage, how does it achieve its effect, how good is it? As long as we confine ourselves to the distinction of aims and processes, the distinction between the two disciplines will be perfectly clear. Confusion enters when we try to extend our distinction to the material handled, and argue that the stuff dredged up by the biographer cannot be relevant to the critics' enquiry. The fact that a biographer is actuated by biographical motives does not mean that he can never turn up a new fact of more than biographical interest. Facts (in this world) tend to be three-dimensional. They can be looked at from different angles. The historian, the scholar, the philologist, all throw up, once in a while, three-dimensional facts which, if they engage our interest, can modify our reading of a work of literature.

V

In arguing for the possible importance of biographical material, I have tried to follow my own advice to choose the invidious example. If such limited investigations can yield critically relevant information, then *a fortiori* how much more may not the history of ideas yield? Here the simple question: 'Do you want to know what the words mean?' (the status of which is disguised in Wimsatt's and Beardsley's essay) should make my point sufficiently clear. The meaning of the word ἀγαθός in Sophocles is supplied by a chapter from the history of ideas. The given meanings of the word 'wit' in the poetry of Pope come to us from the same source. The fact that the critic who has completed his homework on 'background' still has before him the task of following out what Pope does with those meanings does not destroy the relevance of background information as a prerequisite. But, to be sure, Wimsatt and Beardsley have already virtually granted this.

Which makes their analysis of Coffin on Donne all the more puzzling. The lines in question are from the 'Valediction: forbidding Mourning':

> Moving of th' earth brings harmes and feares,
> > Men reckon what it did and meant,
> But trepidation of the spheares,
> > Though greater farre, is innocent.

Coffin interpreted this as a reference to the Copernican hypothesis that the earth goes round the sun, which people found disturbing. Wimsatt and Beardsley, quite rightly dissenting from this view, tell us that Coffin's reading has been perverted by astronomical knowledge, and that the lines go much better if taken, in a commonsense fashion, as Ptolemaic throughout. The irony should be already evident. Wimsatt's and Beardsley's rebuttal of Coffin's use of the history of ideas itself involves the use of history of ideas. Coffin's misinterpretation is not the fault of historicism, it is the fault of

Coffin. It is not just bad criticism, it is bad history of ideas. Conversely, the interpretation of Wimsatt and Beardsley, so far from refuting the claims to critical relevance of the history of ideas, is a reasonably good specimen of it. Wimsatt and Beardsley clearly avail themselves of the information that trepidation of the spheres is, as a translunar phenomenon, in ethical and spiritual contrast with the sublunary character of earthquakes and the like. Moreover I would guess that the very phrase 'trepidation of the spheares' would be virtually meaningless to the average, intelligent man, unlearned in the history of literature and ideas. Ask your bank manager what it means when next you see him.

VI

I am, however, very close to agreement with Wimsatt and Beardsley on one particular, that is, the general critical irrelevance of the author's state of mind at the time of writing. I am not sure, however, that I would erect even this into a principle. I can conceive of a situation in which information about a poet's state of mind (presumably supplied by the poet himself) could supply a richer reading. But to reflect on this point is to realise that the word 'intention' can be understood in two, distinct ways. Here in fact lies the crux of the whole question. I will call these the dualist way and the quasi-behaviorist way. I suspect that there is a confusion of these two ways latent in the following sentence (which occurs near the beginning of Wimsatt's and Beardsley's article):

> How is [the critic] to find out what the poet tried to do? If the poet succeeded in doing it, then the poem itself shows what the poet was trying to do.

Now if the authors hold a dualist view of the nature of intention—if, that is, they think that in every intentional performance there is, first, a pre-existent, identifiably relevant state of mind and, second, an overt action having some appropriate relation to the state of mind—then it seems that the above sentence contains an illegitimate inference. According to the dualist view, success in fulfilling an intention can be measured only by the degree of correspondence between the state of mind and the public action. No-one who was ignorant of the prior state of mind could measure this correspondence.

According to the quasi-behaviorist view, however, we do not need to be admitted to the introspective field of the agent before we decide whether his action is intentional or not; one always has and always will decide such questions by referring to public criteria. Let us suppose that a man is watching, from a window, an armed terrorist advancing up his garden path; he crosses the room, takes down a gun, stations himself where he can see both his sleeping wife and the stranger, waits until the stranger enters the room and draws close to the wife, and at that point shoots him. Should we not say that the husband shot the terrorist intentionally? Yet in reaching this conclusion we have made no reference whatever to what was going on in his head. But now let us suppose that we can, *per impossibile*, see what is happening in the husband's mind. And suppose we discover that what is introspectively available to him is not, e.g., the repeated proposition 'If he gets close I'll shoot him' but simply a series of disconnected images and reflections: 'The light's bad; will dawn come soon? That clock ticks loudly; I may hear the dog bark in a moment.' If we discovered this, would we decide that the husband's action was not intentional after all? I very much doubt it. Indeed, I suspect that in most of the actions quite properly called intentional there need be no corresponding scheme in the mind at all. The man who answers a telephone may have any of a hundred things in his mind as he does so; yet he answers intentionally; certainly not by accident.

VII

I have already asked, in effect, the question which forms the title of this essay. Camus, in *L'Etranger*, showed us how a philosophical novel ought to be written. Instead of the spongy theorising of *La Nausée*, with its ceaseless metaphysical directives to the reader, we are given a *specimen*, a concrete instance minutely and scrupulously observed, for each philosophical reader to construe as he thinks fit. My own question about *L'Etranger* is not the only philosophical question raised by that book. It is not even the most important. It is enough, however, to extricate us from our Wimsattian difficulties.

For Camus has provided precisely the data we require: both the public story and the private one; the steady thread of public action, paid out in the full blaze of the Algerian sun, and the strange, discontinuous lucidity of Meursault's private thoughts. He has even added an actual trial in which we readers can, armed with our special interior knowledge of Meursault, sit beside the jurors of the novel and despise—or not despise—their judgments, reached by such crude external paths. The external story of the killing is pretty simple. Meursault attends the funeral of his mother. His behavior at the ceremony suggests to those who watch that he feels no particular grief at her death. Shortly afterwards he becomes acquainted with a shady character named Raymond Sintès, who asks him to help with a plan. Raymond's scheme is to humiliate his mistress in a peculiarly disgusting manner, by way of revenging her infidelity. It is an essential part of his plan that the mistress be first tricked into a loving repentance, but this can only be brought about by means of a specially eloquent letter 'avec des coups de pied et en même temps des choses pour la faire regretter'. Meursault readily agrees to write this letter for the unliterary Raymond. Raymond's plan is a partial success, although it ends in his beating up the mistress and undergoing an embarrassing interview with the police. A more frightening consequence, however, is that certain Arabs, one of whom is the brother of the girl humiliated by Raymond, begin to make threatening appearances. Meursault learns about this and implicitly ranges himself beside Raymond by promising to warn him if necessary. Later in the story, when the Arabs reappear, Meursault agrees to help his friend if a fight breaks out. A fight follows but proves inconclusive. Meursault is not drawn into it. Some hours after, however, Raymond and Meursault meet the Arabs once more. Meursault, anxious to prevent bloodshed, says '. . . Mais s'il ne sort pas son couteau, tu ne peux pas tirer.'—that is, 'You can't shoot unless he draws his knife.' The implication, clearly, is that if the Arab does draw, you can shoot. A few seconds later, Meursault makes the point clear by adding: 'Prends-le d'homme à homme et donne-moi ton revolver. Si l'autre intervient, ou s'il tire son couteau, je le descendrai.' However, Raymond and Meursault get back safely to the bungalow they are using. Raymond goes inside but Meursault chooses to prowl about outside for a while. It is at this point that he encounters the Arab. Meursault sees the Arab draw his knife and shoots him. After the Arab falls, Meursault fires four more shots into the inert body. The whole incident is played out in intense heat, under a glaring sun. So much for the external story.

Now for the internal: we can pass over Meursault's private feelings at his mother's funeral with the single observation that they do not markedly contradict the conclusions drawn by outside observers. The evidence of the interior story as it relates to Raymond's scheme is again, in a manner, negative. Meursault experiences no repulsion from the idea, entertains no exonerating counter-plot. When we come to the skirmish and the killing, his mind is chiefly filled with a suffocating awareness of heat and light. At one moment only is this distinctly qualified. That is the point at which Meursault tries to restrain Raymond; here, we are told, he feels a real anxiety. The standard English translation by Stuart Gilbert gives another moment—this time a mood of definite, implacable defiance, as Meursault refuses to re-enter the bungalow with Raymond and continues his walk. This, however, rests on an inference from the French 'mes mâchoires se crispaient'; and as such could be contested. To this should be added the negative information that Meursault's state of mind is such that he can perceive no moral distinction between staying or going away, between shooting or not shooting. At the moment of the killing itself, the interior story erupts from its dry, Hemingway style in an explosion of imagery. Meursault, surprised to see the Arab again, grips the gun in his pocket and halts under the fierce sun. The tension rises, and the heat grows more oppressive, reminding Meursault of the heat at his mother's funeral, until at last he irrationally takes a step forward. The Arab at once draws his knife. The light of the sun rebounds from the glittering blade, 'transfixing Meursault's' forehead. Blinded by the glare and deafened by the 'cymbals of the sun', Meursault's grip tightens on the gun. The five shots follow.

These stories, the public and the private, can be reduced to two simple sentences. First, Meursault had armed himself in case something went wrong, and when something did go wrong he fired five times. Second, during the incident his head was full of the light and heat of the sun, of feelings of oppression, flickering anxiety and memory, awareness of a knife drawn before him, desperation. It seems that if we had only the first story to go on we should entertain no doubts about the answer to our title-question. The problem which now rises is this: does the second story exonerate Meursault? Let us take a moment to imagine what *any* close account of the introspective accompaniment of a murder—not an accidental killing—would be like. To my mind, the answer after we have scrutinized the interior account remains unchanged. Although there is room for argument about the degree of responsibility involved, Meursault's action was, in the ordinary sense of the word, an intentional performance. I thus opt for the 'quasi-behaviorist' view (which obviously owes more than a little to Professor Gilbert Ryle).

VIII

To take once again the invidious instance: even when I am trying to decide whether an action *of my own* was intentional or not, I do not necessarily proceed by looking for a particular state of mind. If I ask myself, 'Did I intend to contradict that man so bluntly?' I find myself searching, not for a memory of an inwardly framed project: 'Now contradict him', but rather for memories of the precise tenor of our conversation, was I pressed for time, had *he* just contradicted me? There is, I suppose, a sense in which this *is* scrutinizing my own state of mind, but, if so, it is a surprisingly Rylean sense.

But perhaps I should fight one more round before I leave the point. Often an attempt to remember whether an action was intentional or not will take the form not of a search for an appropriate previous mental state but simply of an effort to remember whether or not one was surprised by what happened. Here it might be objected that the word 'surprise' betrays my case. 'Surprise', it will be said, 'occurs when the event contradicts the expectation, that is, what you think will happen—in fact, the previous mental state. Your antithesis between the search for a previous mental state on the one hand and the attempt to discover whether or not one was surprised on the other accordingly collapses, since the very word "surprise" presupposes a reference to a previous mental state.' My reply is as follows: it is doubtful whether an 'expectation' is necessarily, or even usually, the sort of introspectible phenomenon which your argument requires. Often enough we become conscious of an expectation only when it disappointed. Thus I should be surprised if I saw a dog on the roof of the National Gallery. This would, in a perfectly normal sense, be contrary to my expectation. But this does not mean that all the way from Victoria to Trafalgar Square I was saying to myself, 'There will be no dog on the roof of the National Gallery'. The fact that the National Gallery never entered my head would not mean that the surprise was not a surprise, nor would it mean that I lied if I said 'That's unexpected!' 'Expectation' is not typically the name of a conscious mental state; it is a word which is useful in situations where a course of rational action has been interrupted, or in some way intruded upon. It follows that my antithesis between looking for a mental state and looking for a surprise should be allowed to stand.

IX

Let us now look again at Wimsatt's and Beardsley's observation that if a poet succeeds in fulfilling his intention the poem itself will show it. Clearly, the quasi-behaviorist can make sense of this: an action is intentional when it makes sense, when one part rationally precedes another; that is what 'intentional' *means*. A poetic effect is intentional when it hangs together, when it *goes*; that is what 'intentional' *means*. But if Wimsatt and Beardsley avail themselves of this saving interpretation, it can only be at the cost of sacrificing their main contention, The Intentional Fallacy would cease, forthwith, to be fallacious. On this hypothesis it makes perfectly good sense to ask 'What did Shakespeare intend here?' where 'intend' will be explained in terms of the coherence, the movement and order of the images and ideas *as expressed*, and will have nothing to do with the question 'What was streaming through Shakespeare's consciousness at six p.m. on the 14th November 1604?' To say 'Keats clearly intended x' is as simple as to say 'The train-robbers clearly intended y'.

The same analysis could, naturally, be applied to *The Personal Heresy*

(1939) by C. S. Lewis and E. M. W. Tillyard, an earlier version of the same controversy. Tillyard maintained that the proper object of the critic's attention in reading *Paradise Lost* is the mind of the poet. Lewis replied that he cared little for Milton's *mind*, being more interested in angels, devils and the movement of the poem. 'Mind' is here ambiguous in exactly the same way as 'intention'. If 'mind' means 'Milton's stream of consciousness from second to second', Lewis is right. If it means all the marvelous things that Milton said and wrote, or might say or write, then Tillyard's right; but only tautologously right in that his position could now be expressed in the following form: 'We read Milton in order to read Milton—all the ideas and images of his poetry'.

What about consulting the poet himself? My position on this follows from my position on ordinary intention. There are some hyper-Ryleans who hold that a man is no better judge of what he intends than an outsider is; that the knowledge is identical in kind in either case. There are others who hold that a man's statement that he intended a thing is in principle not corrigible since *ex hypothesi* the agent is the unique authority. I reject both these extremes and suggest that the agent has a special but not indisputable access to his own actions. Similarly, the poet is in an especially good position for watching the movement of a poem, but his judgments on it are not infallible. So, if in doubt, why *not* ask the poet? He could help.

DAVID SPRINTZEN

The Stranger

> A man devoid of hope and conscious
> of being so has ceased to belong to the
> future, and no gospel keeps its
> meaning for him.

WHO IS THIS STRANGER?

"Mother died today. Or maybe it was yesterday, I don't know. I received a telegram from the rest home: MOTHER DECEASED. BURIAL TOMORROW. VERY TRULY YOURS. It doesn't say anything. Maybe it was yesterday." Not exactly the normal reaction of a son to the news of his mother's death. What kind of person responds in this matter-of-fact way? Are we not at first put off by such casualness? Perhaps even scandalized by our initial encounter with Patrice Meursault?

Is not this Meursault a stranger to our normal feelings and expectations? We sense a distance. Not that he seeks to scandalize or offend. Far from it. He is rather quite unassuming, almost shy. He wants neither to offend nor to be hated. Expressing an air of naïveté, he often experiences an undercurrent of uneasiness as to what is expected of him. Occasionally he is

From *Camus: A Critical Examination.* © 1988 Temple University.

moved to apologize without quite knowing what he is guilty of. When asking his boss for two days off to attend his mother's funeral, for example, he feels that he "ought not to have said that to him." Or, when sensing the reproach of the director of the rest home, he begins to explain himself.

A subtle tension thus pervades our relation with Meursault from the first. Between the complete unassuming naturalness of his actions and observations, on the one hand, and his insensitivity to normal feelings and expectations, on the other, a gulf emerges that makes it quite difficult for us to coordinate our emotional response to him. We are drawn to identify, even sympathize, with him. And yet how can we not feel a condemnation begin to arise within us to which we are not yet able to give expression?

In short, we are disoriented, perhaps even slightly offended, by our encounter with a being who shows no sign of sharing normal human feelings. Nor does he attest to any normal aspirations. Slowly we are familiarized with his world, even led to see our own world through his eyes. Stripped of our normal "conceptual lenses," we see that world increasingly as arbitrary, capricious, pretentious, even hypocritical. By the time of the trial we may even find ourselves tempted, if not actually inclined, to side with Meursault against the prosecutor and jurists who inhabit the world that was ours at the beginning of the novel. However short-lived that experiential voyage may prove to be, the stylistic accomplishment is remarkable.

Perhaps Meursault is Camus's portrait of the being he might have become had not M. Germain, to whom he dedicated his Nobel Prize address, rescued him from the life of physical plenitude and spiritual exhaustion that was the lot of lower-class French Algerian youth. Recall Camus's friend Vincent, mentioned in "Summer in Algiers," whose direct and uncomplicated lifestyle and morals, though lacking in love, suggest a closeness to the vital and sensuous qualities of existence. Meursault resides in that shrunken present rich with sensations that lead nowhere. But that must not be misunderstood. He is not without feelings or morals. He feels for Salamano, is moved by the testimony of Celeste, and feels concern for several individuals, including the magistrate. Throughout his ordeal, he treats everyone with consideration and is even able to see the point of view of the prosecutor. He simply refuses to interpret his experience or to give it a significance beyond what is immediately present to the senses.

A lively sensitivity to the play of light and shadow colors his day. The weather, qualitative changes in experience and in the modulations of nature practically enrapture him. He takes them as they are, asking and expecting nothing more. At the same time he remains practically blind to the socially established meanings with which others embellish events.

Nowhere is this more evident than in his relation with Marie. Like

Vincent, he knows nothing of love and cares nothing for the institution of marriage. But when Marie smiles in a certain way he is attracted to her and wants her. His desires are not without warmth, but they lack premeditation or foresight. They are spontaneous responses to sensuous qualities and reflect little if any conceptual interpretation or social propriety.

The fascination of Meursault and the young journalist with one another may also be seen in this light. Camus became a journalist as a result of having by chance had Louis Germain as his teacher. And so with the novel. Had Meursault not been compelled by familial poverty to give up his education and abandon his career aspirations, he might have found himself in the audience covering a murder trial. Thus their fascination with each other suggests the chance nature of their destinies and their reciprocal being for one another. In the journalist Meursault sees the person he might have become, fascinated with the person the journalist Camus might have been.

And similarly with the problems of poverty with which Camus's early sensibilities were clearly marked. For it is poverty that keeps Patrice Meursault from pursuing his education and would have done likewise for young Albert. The testimony of his friends about never being invited into his home bears witness to an anguished sensitivity, as does his evocative discussion of the novel *La Douleur*, which had such a profound impact upon him. Camus's first effort at a full-length novel, *A Happy Death*, is quite explicit on the destiny of those condemned to poverty, whatever the natural gifts of their environment. Without money with which to buy the time to be happy, *that* Meursault would have been condemned to the exhausting rigors and spiritual depletion of the 9-to-5 job, which, however necessary to make ends meet, leads only to a wasted life and meaningless "natural death."

Who then is this Patrice Meursault who so innocently disconcerts us? A clerk without ambition, who rejects his boss's offer of advancement and a position in Paris. A man who will marry Marie if she wishes, but who considers marriage no big deal. Obviously intelligent, but having been compelled by poverty to give up schooling, he concluded that ambition was a waste of time and effort. All that mattered was living one day at a time, accepting the pleasures offered, and expecting no more.

Having given up the future, his life follows the trajectory of the moment: job, acquaintances, social routines, climate. Even his language, with its simple factual statements, its lack of connectives, its concentration on sensations and images, bears witness to the pervasiveness of the present. Events happen and Patrice responds. Camus observes: "He limits himself to *responding to questions*. At first, these are the questions which the world asks us every day—[at the end] they are the chaplain's questions. Thus, I define my character negatively."

Such is the person we encounter at the outset. It is not clear what effect the death of his mother had on him. Judging by his explicit response, it would seem to have had no effect, other than to mildly annoy his employer and thus cause some discomfort for Patrice. Yet it is here that the narrative begins. The opening lines suggest that Meursault began writing the chronicle shortly after receiving the note from the rest home—perhaps as a diary or a random collection of notes. The exact status of the narrative is not clear or consistent. Pursuing internal clues would lead one to conclude either that he kept a running account of his life from then on, making somewhat regular entries after the day's or week's events, or that everything was essentially written from the perspective of a post-sentence reevaluation of his life. Or perhaps it is simply an oral report of his life given at sporadic moments to an impartial observer. In any case, the entries in the first part of the narrative tend to be more direct, more in the style of an immediate, noninterpretative reporting of events in temporal sequence, whereas those of the second part involve greater editorial selectivity. If we take seriously this change in perspective as the narrative proceeds, we would probably be led to a conclusion emphasizing its temporal elaboration. In any case, the world we see is the world Patrice is conscious of seeing *as he sees it*. The meaning of these events is, in the first instance, the meaning of these events *to him*. And it is to that meaning that I now turn.

Meursault's World

What then is the world that is revealed to us through this stranger's eyes? One in which events just happen. Of course, a habitual pattern carries us from day to day. But there does not seem to be any logic to the pattern. "Rising, streetcar, four hours in the office or the factory, meal, streetcar, four hours of work, meal, sleep, and Monday Tuesday Wednesday Thursday Friday and Saturday according to the same rhythm." Expressions, movements, modes of dressing and of carrying oneself strike the observer as do colors, lights, sounds, and temperature. Social and natural events merge and interpenetrate, without priority or distinction between them. The social is rather but an aspect of the natural. There is but one unitary present, with the world of habit being altogether natural and inevitable for Meursault.

It is from this perspective that the world is revealed to us in the first part of the narrative. Nothing significant seems to happen. Each event takes place on the same metaphysical plane. If one thing is singled out for attention rather than another, that is only because it momentarily grabbed Patrice's attention. No hierarchies of value are recognized. Occasional lyrical passages relieve the emotional tedium like shafts of radiant sunlight bursting through the skies of an otherwise overcast day. But that is their only significance. Each of the first five chapters concludes essentially with the observation "that, after all, nothing had changed."

With the killing of the Arab, however, "it all began." Meursault understood that with that shot he "had broken the harmony of the day, the marvelous silence of a beach where [he] had been happy." The natural order is shattered. The cyclical time of a habitual life immersed in nature is transfigured by a single event. All later events now take on the meaning of either leading up to or following from it. If the metaphysical ground of the first part is cyclical nature, that of the second is historicized nature, nature subjected to the organization and interpretation of society. Rather than eternal repetition, events now become the children of the past and the parents of the future, in a linear history that leads either to death or to transfiguration. Each life becomes a unique journey, each event a transition. This metaphysical transformation demands an appropriate existential one. Patrice can no longer act as if his life will be eternal repetition. The unity of nature and history is sundered, and historically socialized reason emerges to insist on a different kind of accounting.

Under the pressure of events, this realization begins to dawn on Patrice. First, in jail, he is called upon to recount the events at the beach. He is questioned about his past and initially draws a blank, noting that he has lost the habit of self-interrogation. Thinking about his past is the beginning of an experiential transformation by which he comes to locate himself in a linear historical world, which location is the precondition of his being able to take personal responsibility for his life.

With this dawning recollection of his past, a sense of perspective emerges. The flatness of the experiential landscape undergoes seismic transformation. Preferences are recognized and valued. An emerging selectivity stylistically transforms the narrative. Criteria of value are suggested. The sensually given is subject to reflective appraisal, and the previously implicit ethics of quantity begins to acquire an appreciation of experiential qualities that only conscious attention can bring. This qualitative self-appropriation of life comes to consummation in the encounter with the chaplain, when the values by which Meursault had lived are reflectively articulated and defended. Thus completes the reconstruction of his experience. From the reconstitution of his memory to the reaffirmation of his life, Meursault has achieved a reflective grasp of the life he has lived, and has found that it was good. He has also realized that to have so lived was to have rejected the expectations of the established social order. Thus a de facto rebel becomes a de jure one. An explicit articulation of these emerging values confronts a chaplain who embodies the rejected order. But I am jumping ahead of my story.

The world was initially composed of natural and social habits—habits of things and of people. Each had its regularity and its unique sensuousness. Patrice observes and responds. He never asks why, what ought to be done, although he does comment upon connections between events—why, for example, the people in the streets on Sunday behave as they do. He thus reveals an ability to analyze facts for their connections, but no interest in exploring purposes or goals. Occasionally he notes the purposes of others— as with Raymond's desire to get even—but for him, and for us through his eyes, this is but another fact that he observes and to which he responds.

Social conventions also lose their privileged status and appear not to differ from natural occurrences. Like voyagers from another planet, we are often left to wonder at the natives' strange behavior, their dance of social etiquette and the mirage of their personal beliefs. A feeling of purposelessness textures the narrative, pervading Part 1. A feeling of strangeness is subliminally generated in the reader by the contrast between the pure contingency of the events recounted and our subterranean sense of their familiarity and ordinary meaningfulness. This contrast is brought explicitly to the fore in Part 2 by the establishment's insistence on the purposefulness of its world. "The meaning of the book consists precisely in the parallelism of the two parts," affirmed Camus

The use of the disconnected compound past (*passé composé*)—of which so much has been made in critical studies since Sartre's "Explication de l'Etranger"—tends to reduce each fact to an irreducible and unconnected given, thus strengthening this emerging sense of the absurdity of the human situation when it lacks any aspiration to order. Clearly this is Camus's intention. That our world is governed by chance is brought home so much more forcefully when presented by and realized in the life of one who is so unassumingly natural and unself-conscious. A simple individual, without depth or contrivance, presents our world to us in a way that reveals it as being without deeper significance. Confronting such a world tends to make people uncomfortable. "Do you want my life to have no meaning?" the magistrate cries. Whatever his intentions, Patrice's way of living is felt as threatening to society's institutions, beliefs, and aspirations.

Estrangement

The social order from which Meursault is so estranged is the world of ambition and the desire for advancement that his employer expects, as well as the decorum and grief to which all at the burial bear witness. It is the wearing of black as a show of mourning, and the sustained sadness that forbids the beginning of a liaison on the day following the burial of one's mother, not to say the sacrilege of viewing a Fernandel film. It is also the expectation that one ought to cry at the funeral of one's grandmother, about which Camus personally felt such conflict and hypocrisy. And it is certainly viewing love as a serious matter and treating marriage as an important social institution. Here we glimpse the deeper social meaning to which normal people cling with ferocious tenacity. The rituals and ceremonies, the institutions and practices, by which society daily reenacts the drama of its cosmic significance are grounded in a system of values and beliefs that give shape to a living that might otherwise hover precariously close to the abyss of nothingness. Not to speak of the offices, hierarchies, and prerogatives by which the power and self-esteem of the few may be protected from the desires of the many.

The personal appropriation of that ritualized belief system defines and valorizes an individual's place, giving us our sense of what it is important to do, to strive after, to avoid, and to become. People act in the belief that some things matter more than others, and because they feel that it is worth the effort. This is quite normal. Precisely so.

Meursault had in fact given up on these beliefs when he gave up his ambition. We can take him to have been an intelligent working-class French Algerian whose social development was short-circuited by the need to leave school and get a job. We may even conjecture that this necessity followed upon an upbringing in which circumstances—perhaps including his more than average intelligence—had conspired to keep him somewhat apart from others, not fully integrated into social norms and practices. All this might of course have described Camus himself to some extent.

In any case, giving up ambition and, by implication, the belief system by which it is sustained, Meursault settles into a style of life in which inarticulate personal needs and satisfactions dictate spontaneous responses to the demands of nature and others. He goes along with the flow of habits and events. Such is the path of least resistance, except when his inclination moves him otherwise. And why act differently when "it's all the same to him"?

But then the beach, where "the trigger gave way [and Meursault] . . . understood that [he] had broken the harmony of the day, the marvellous silence of a beach where [he] had been happy. Then [he] pulled the trigger four more times on the motionless corpse where the bullets buried themselves effortlessly. And it was as if, with these four brief shots, [he] was knocking on the door of misfortune." What could have been simpler or more natural? Heat, exhaustion, the beating of the sun, the shaft of light, the threatening confrontation—and the body tightens up to defend itself: The hand clenches the revolver, and the trigger gives way. With perhaps a touch of exasperation, even annoyance, at the intrusion of the threatening other into this already oppressive situation, the tension previously held coiled within his body bursts forth with those four fatal shots, as if it had been waiting for that moment of release.

All of which is, in one sense, no great deal. Oppressive conditions give rise to tension. The tension is released, and life goes on. Yet a person was killed. Surprisingly perhaps, the authorities initially show little interest in Meursault. As they become aware of his strangeness, their attitude changes. He does not "live by the rules." He does not think like ordinary people. He does not pay his respects, but seems indifferent to everything that is usually taken seriously. Is not such an attitude offensive? Who is this person, to treat cavalierly what we hold so dear? How can he act this way? There must be something the matter with him. Otherwise there would have to be something the matter with us for taking so seriously that which is not worthy of such respect. If we can't get him to see the error of his ways, thus acknowledging the Truth of ours, we must treat him as a traitor to the human community, and make him pay for his transgression.

Thus a transformed portrait of Meursault emerges. Initially he had simply appeared to be a bit odd, certainly not offensive or brutish. But he didn't want to see his mother's body, he smoked at her funeral, he rejected a chance to move to Paris, and he didn't take marriage seriously. He even seemed inordinately sensitive to trivial matters but awkward, even dense about the norms of social behavior. Now that queerness becomes perversity, indifference metamorphoses into insensitivity, and passivity into calculated criminality. No longer will Meursault's life be allowed to follow the trajectory of inclination and habit. The socialized demand for coherence and purposefulness now takes control. What may well have been lurking in the background now takes center stage, insisting that events conform to its terms. The portrait of a coldblooded, ruthless murderer takes shape. And why *did* Meursault fire those four extra shots into the body of a corpse, asks the prosecutor, if not to make sure that the job was well done?

Returning to the beach and Meursault's description of what took place, the *why* seems about as relevant as asking a plant why it grows toward the light. Genetics, habit, and inclination seem sufficient. The *why* presupposes a world of purposeful beings who act for more or less premeditated reasons. But is that what took place on the beach?

> I walked slowly toward the rocks and it felt like my forehead was
> swelling and pulsating under the sun. All this heat pressed down
> on me. . . . I gritted my teeth, clenched my fists in my pants
> pockets. . . . My jaws would contract with every sword-like

reflexion that darted up from the sand, from a bleached shell, or from a piece of broken glass. . . .

As soon as [the Arab] saw me, he raised up a little and put one hand in his pocket. Naturally my hand closed around Raymond's revolver which I hadn't removed from my jacket. . . . A whole beach vibrating with the sun was surging behind me. I took a few steps toward the source. . . . The scorching sun attacked my cheeks and I felt drops of sweat forming in my eyebrows. It was the same sun as on the day I had buried Mother and, as then, my forehead hurt and all my veins were pulsating underneath my skin. Because of this heat which I could no longer stand, I took a step forward. . . . The Arab took out his knife and pointed it at me in the sun. The light flashed on the steel and it was like a long blade attacking me on the forehead. At the same instant, the sweat that had been forming in my eyebrows ran down all at once over my pupils, covering them with a warm, thick veil. . . . I felt nothing more then but the cymbals of sun on my forehead, and, indistinctly, the bursting blade of light from the sword continually in front of me. This burning sword was eating away at my eyelids and digging into my aching eyes. It was then that everything reeled. . . . It seemed to me that the heavens had opened to their full extent in order to let it rain fire. My entire being became tight and I closed my grip on the revolver. The trigger gave way.

No interpretation, no motive, no conscious revolt is apparent. Only the quasi-instinctive, perhaps physiological, response of a natural animal to an oppressive situation. Under the pressure of the sun, he tenses up and the trigger yields. The Arab, the sun's rays striking off the blade of the knife, the taut grasp of the revolver—all are part of one natural environment whose elements are in tension with one another. Whom can one ask for a motive? The environment is returned to equilibrium by the removal of a nexus of tension. That is all.

But Meursault is a human being and a member of society, and its officials soon see that much more is at stake than simply the killing of an Arab by a French Algerian—about which, it should be noted, little official concern was likely to have been expressed at that time. "For the magistrate," writes Barrier, in his perceptive study of The Stranger, "a consciousness which is so non-human represents the grave threat of dismantling the entire edifice of values upon which the very order of society is based."

Two points should be noted here. Meursault is portrayed as a brute, a person so cold and calculating as to smoke at his mother's funeral, begin a liaison on the following day, and commit pre-meditated murder without the least feeling of remorse. Such a "moral monster" would of course be a threat to any order. But Meursault is still more threatening, for he does not even recognize, not to say acknowledge, the values and norms by which the fabric of society is woven together. If he would repent and admit guilt, he would at least implicitly legitimize the claim of those values. Even a murderer can be pardoned—far more easily, Camus suggests, than one who not only refuses to acknowledge social norms, but fails even to perceive their existence. His refusal thus constitutes a sort of inarticulate metaphysical rejection by which he places himself beyond the horizon of the normal social world. As a spiritual alien upon whom accepted social absolutes make no claim, his being can only appear to the "good people" as a threat to the values and beliefs that are dear to them.

But why, one might ask, must the officials insist upon portraying Meursault as a ruthless killer, one who is morally guilty of matricide? Why must such evil motives be imputed to him in the first place? Why must society—in the persons of the magistrate, defense attorney, and prosecutor—refuse in principle to see him as he is?

We might reflect here upon the problem faced by the early Christians who had to come to terms with the Jews' rejection of Christ as the Messiah. With unbelieving pagans a more energetic propagation of the faith would have sufficed. But the challenge posed by the Jews was of another order. To them the revelation had been given. How can one account for the rejection of a faith that seems both self-evident and salvific? If Christians were not to doubt their faith's evidence, truth, or significance, what were they to make of the Jews' rejection? Either the Jews were ignorant innocents—like children or, perhaps, brutes—or they were willful, insensitive, and possibly downright evil.

Similarly, Meursault is too intelligent to be dismissed as a fool, but his attitude directly challenges the certainty with which the established order confronts the cosmic abyss. By imputing an evil nature to him, the prosecutor can both bring him within the normal cosmic drama and explain the specific reason for his behavior. Let's look at this logic. "To understand is, above all, to unify. The mind's deepest desire, even in its most elaborate operations, parallels man's unconscious feeling in the face of his universe; it is an insistence upon familiarity, an appetite for clarity. Understanding the world for a man is reducing it to the human, stamping it with his seal."

A motive, no matter how malevolent, bespeaks an intelligible individual. A motivated act is an intelligible act; its world, a familiar world. To insist upon there being a motive—to insist so unself-consciously that the possibility that there might not be one does not *even* arise—while, at the same time, characterizing that motive as the willful rejection of humane sensibilities, here truly is the "best of all possible worlds." Presented with a criminal who is meta-physically comprehensible but morally reprehensible, society may, at one and the same time, reaffirm its cosmic drama and purge itself momentarily of any repressed and taboo inclinations that threaten to shatter it.

What would it mean to accept Meursault as he presents himself? How would we make sense of a world in which chance was pervasive, and in which natural processes predominated to no purpose? Would not a recognition of the essential arbitrariness of the social order and its hierarchies circumscribe the domain of meaning, rendering it contingent and without direction? And what of the "justice" system? And the organization of power and social prerogatives? Is it any wonder that an "evil" Meursault is more intelligible and less threatening than a impulsive one?

> A world that can be explained even with bad reasons is a familiar world. . . . On the other hand, in a universe suddenly divested of illusions and light, man feels an alien, a stranger. His exile is without remedy since he is deprived of the memory of a lost home or the hope of a promised land. This divorce between man and his life, the actor and his setting, is properly the feeling of absurdity.

Meursault is thus inadvertently the most dangerous of rebels, for he rejects the metaphysical foundation of normal social order. As a de facto rebel who becomes conscious of his rebellion only at the end, he must be "put in his place." Society must either obtain his complicity or his destruction. That is the way with absolutes. They brook no opposition.

Barrier correctly observes that for Camus "Meursault is innocent of the *moral* crime of which he is accused and the society guilty for condemning him for such a crime." Rather, Meursault's revolt, involving as it does a reaffirmation of the manner in which he lived his life, contains for Camus elements essential to the establishment and maintenance of human dignity.

Consciousness and Death

Having been indicted for "not playing the game," Meursault will no longer be allowed to freely follow the flow of his feelings. Viewed as a criminal, he will learn deprivation. At first, quite naturally his attention turns toward his immediate surroundings. But that is not long sustaining. Cut off from the world, he is forced back upon himself. Robbed of access to space, and confronted with the fact that he can no longer take the future for granted, he begins to think about his past life—and especially Marie.

With the slow awakening of his memory, a new depth of being emerges. He begins to appear as a being "for himself." Rather than just being there, his life appears as something to be lived, valued, retained, reconstituted, reaffirmed, and, perhaps, redirected. It is to be reflectively taken in hand, to be consciously molded in accord with his personal evaluation of what matters. Memory fuels self-consciousness, as habituated passivity gives way to lucid affirmation. This subterranean transition develops throughout Part 2, reaching its culmination in the encounter with the chaplain. At first, he is called upon to recount his life. Repeatedly he must retell the story of the beach confrontation. Then, as days turn into weeks and months, the rhythm of the days fades into the monotony of an unchanging present. With the turn inward, the being that he is "for himself" begins to emerge, fascinating him. He finds a reflected image of himself in a mirror. He is drawn to the journalist who suggests the being he might have been. The automaton woman reappears—that being who is completely other than himself—and there seems to be a mutual fascination with each other: she, for whom every action is rationally precalculated and purposeful; he, for whom none had been. It is as if the journalist and the automaton woman are the mirrors wherein Meursault may see the range of beings he might have been.

As Meursault comes to self-awareness, the narrative undergoes stylistic transformation. In place of the seemingly unedited description of chance events in temporal order, we now have the selective reporting of particular events. Long periods are now condensed into a few paragraphs, while a single significant day requires its own chapter. Important encounters are presented in detail, while others drift into obscurity. And judgments emerge, almost unintentionally. But it is the encounter with the chaplain following the condemnation to death that is required to make this existential transformation explicit.

Without doubt the thought of death can remarkably concentrate one's attention. Today and tomorrow can be taken as they come only so long as one expects them to keep coming. Once the death sentence is handed down, the image of the guillotine looms over our horizon, threatening decisively to sever our relation with our future possibilities. And so with Patrice.

> No matter how hard I tried to persuade myself, I could not accept that insolent certitude. Because, in the final analysis, it came to a disproportion between the judgment on which the certitude was based and its imperturbable course, from the moment when this judgment had been pronounced. The fact that the sentence had been read at eight o'clock rather than at five, that it might have been something entirely different . . . it

seemed to me that all of this took away from the seriousness of
such a verdict.

And yet, however chancy the process leading up to the judgment,
"from the second it had been given, its effects became as sure, as serious" as
the most palpable and inescapable of facts.

Doubtless, there is something absurd in the disproportion between the
haphazard and contingent nature of daily existence and the certainty of the
punishment's execution. Confronted with this absurdity, Meursault's initial
response is typical.

> What interests me just now is if I can avoid the machine, if there
> can be a way to escape the unavoidable. . . . I don't know how
> many times I've asked myself if there are any cases of condemned
> men who were able to fool the machine, who were able to disap-
> pear before the execution. . . . I scolded myself for not having
> paid enough attention to the accounts of executions. . . . There,
> perhaps, I might have found accounts of escape. I would have
> learned that in at least one case, the wheel had stopped, that in
> its never-ceasing momentum, hazard and chance, one time only,
> had caused a change in the normal order of things. One time! In
> a way, I believe that would have sufficed for me.

Patrice is struggling here to find grounds for the "leap of faith." Faced
directly with death, his passionate will to live becomes explicit in his search
for a way out. "What mattered was the possibility of escape, of being able to
jump out of the path of inevitability, a crazy course which offered all chances
of hope." Here, through his struggle, we encounter the fundamentals of the
human condition that constitute the problematic of *The Myth*.

Only after having confronted the facts of his impending execution will
he allow himself the luxury of hoping that his appeal might be granted. That
thought let loose a "surge of blood that ran through my body, causing tears
to come to my eyes. I needed to work at moderating my cries of ecstasy, to
reason with them so to speak."

It is precisely at such a moment that the chaplain entered, after having
thrice been rejected by Meursault. This missionary for Jesus, who exudes the
self-satisfaction of those who "know" themselves to be "in the Truth," incar-
nates a religious hope built upon acquiescence in the sacrifice of innocence.
For the nonbeliever, however, who feels the full weight of finitude bearing
down upon him, the chaplain's complacent acquiescence in, and even
complicity with, this capricious and unjust order of things is ultimately

unbearable. Having struggled vainly to reconcile two contradictory visions of his future, Meursault's outrage finally coalesces in an explosive rejection of rationalized unjustice. As the chaplain literally pins Patrice to the wall, chastising him for his attachment to this life, and challenging him to deny that he had come to hope for another, de facto rebellion finds articulate expression, retrospectively justifying his previous life. Having made explicit the link between the leap of faith and the rejection of life, Meursault can no longer contain the rage welling up within him. The only after-life for which he could hope would be "a life where I could remember this one." No, the chaplain was not his "father: he was with the others." And what is this "truth" he is offering but a path of illusions built upon renunciation? Meursault will not acquiesce in this life-denying myth. His truth had been of this earth, and it will remain so.

He had lived by the impassioned and transitory values of this life. "I had been right. I was still right." So what if they were finite? He had not been wrong. He may have failed to reflectively appreciate the life he had lived. He may have let that life slide along, rather than consciously giving shape to it. But he had not betrayed it. If he had lived in a way that involved de facto alienation from social norms, *that* had not been a mistake. "Far from his being deprived of all sensitivity, a profound, because tenacious, passion animate[d] him." He had glimpsed a truth that involved rejection of normalized hypocrisy. "It was but a negative truth—the truth of being and feeling— but one without which no conquest over self or world will ever be possible."

It thus becomes clear what Camus meant when he referred to Meursault as the sole Christ we deserve today. For this sacrificial figure's innocence is born out of social and even metaphysical naïveté, upon which altar he will be crucified. Unlike Jesus, however, who can accept his death in resignation, asking his father to "forgive them for they know not what they do," Meursault rejects such resignation. Acceptance of the unjust suffering of innocents—for Camus, the rock upon which Peter's church is built—can be counterposed to the revolt that bursts forth like a mighty stream, drowning the chaplain in its righteous indignation and passionate reaffirmation. Perhaps it makes sense for one who believes in a salvific afterlife to be so forgiving, but that makes only more poignant the loss of this life for which Meursault can find no redeeming features. Resignation and forgiveness only add insult to injury, compounding injustice with complicity. No, rather than forgiving them, Patrice wants his revolt confirmed in the cries of hatred with which he hopes to be greeted by a crowd of spectators on the day of his execution.

From the death of his mother to his impending execution, passing through his killing of the Arab and society's condemnation of him, *The*

Stranger reveals a more sophisticated development of that transition from natural to conscious death that had been the basic structure of *A Happy Death*. What could be more natural for Meursault than the dying of an elderly woman who had lived out her life? Thus his response. But such nonchalance with respect to natural processes leaves us totally prey to chance and to the dissolution of human meanings. Thus the death of the Arab, but one more natural event for Meursault. And yet, it was by his hand that the trigger was pulled, a point of which the authorities make much. Consciousness was a participant in and contributor to this death, even if only by inadvertence. Such will *not* be the case for society. It intends consciously and quite deliberately to kill Meursault for transgressing the moral bounds of its world. For these bounds constitute society's response to the existential challenge of finitude. However unjust this sentence, the chaplain intercedes on behalf of accepting it as the price that must be paid if belief in the transcendent significance of human life is to be sustained. Patrice rebels so vehemently because death is not an entree into another life but the end of this one, and we should not so easily acquiesce in its realization. Death will come, inevitably, but we need not—must not—assist it. Not by inadvertence and certainly not by conscious decision. As for rational justification of such complicity, that is an evil of another order. We must rather draw forth from this dawning recognition of human finitude a renewed appreciation for what life has to offer. A passionate will "to exhaust the field of the possible" must replace our "longing for immortal heights."

A Cryptomythic Tale

If Meursault is not guilty of murder, nevertheless a human being *is* dead and Meursault *did* pull the trigger. Although not guilty of having *willed* the slaying, he *is* guilty of permitting himself to become an accessory in the destruction of a human life. Actually, his guilt seems to lie precisely in his *not* having willed anything. Lacking lucidity, Camus seems to be suggesting, we are ever in danger of entering into complicity with the forces of destruction. Consider the drama of "The Misunderstanding" or the citizens of Oran at the onset of *The Plague*. Human revolt at this stage of Camus's development primarily consists in the struggle to maintain a lucid awareness of our condition. Meursault at the crucial moment fails to take control of himself, to maintain the necessary human distance from the forces of nature. He succumbs passively to union with nature—at the expense of the human.

This failure is similar in source to the temptation that Camus speaks of in his contemporaneous essay "The Minotaur, or the Stop at Oran."

The Minotaur is boredom. . . . These are the lands of innocence. But innocence needs sand and stones. And man has forgotten how to live among them. At least it seems so, for he has taken refuge in this extraordinary city where boredom sleeps. Nevertheless, that very confrontation constitutes the value of Oran. The capital of boredom . . . is surrounded by an army in which every stone is a soldier. In the city, and at certain hours . . . what a temptation to identify oneself with those stones, to melt into that burning and impassive universe that defies history and its ferments! That is doubtless futile. But there is in every man a profound instinct which is neither that of destruction nor that of creation. It is merely a matter of resembling nothing.

The stranger, it might be thought, bespeaks an inner call of our being, a countercultural invitation to return to a precivilized innocence, free of the burdens of individuality and conscience. One might think here of Freud's death instinct, the purported desire to return to our inorganic origins that constituted for Freud such a profound threat to the requirements of civilized living. Freud is, of course, not alone in speculating upon such presocial needs, desires, or longings. Whatever their scientific warrant, the pervasiveness of attention to them suggests that these reflections are giving expression, however inadequate the form, to very significant human concerns. At an archetypal level, Meursault might remind us of Rousseau's noble savage, whose innocence has not yet been sullied by sophistication and social pretention. There is, however, a price to be paid for such natural innocence, of which both the killing and society's response give us a sense.

Two further points about the dramatic significance of this crypto-mythic tale need to be noted. First, there seems to be some ambiguity in the novel concerning the positive aspects of Meursault's character. Many have taken him to be bored with, and generally indifferent to, living. Certainly he shows no enthusiasm for all those futures we hold so dear. Similarly for matters of social etiquette. At the same time, he is fascinated by the behavior of the automaton woman—to the extent of trying to follow her when she leaves the restaurant—while he carefully attends to events at the home, at the trial, or, on Sundays, in the street in front of his balcony. Further, he evinces an enthusiasm for swimming, for hopping on the truck to take off for the port with Emmanuel, and, of course, for Marie Cardona. The "normal" reading of his character as indifferent to life may tell us more about the readers than about the person being interpreted. Such a reading of Meursault may be further confirmation of the extent to which we readers predicate the significance of *our* lives on the meaningfulness of belief systems that are being placed in question by him. Thus we would be finding him guilty in a manner similar to that of the jurors.

Whether or not Camus is successful in making this point, however, his intent should not be in doubt. "Meursault is not . . . a derelict for me, but a poor and naked man, in love with the sun which leaves no shadows. Far from his being deprived of all sensitivity, a profound, because tenacious, passion animates him, the passion for the absolute and for truth. *It concerns a truth which remains negative*, the truth of being and feeling, *but one without which no conquest of self and world will ever be possible*" (my italics).

The second point concerns the mythic significance of Oran. Given the previous description of the quality of Oranian life, the selection of Oran as the location for the outbreak of plague should not come as a surprise. The citizens of Oran, in their passive innocence, their boredom, their lack of lucidity, succumb to the temptations of habit. They are a sort of collective Meursault without the inarticulate passion, captives of the forces of nature and habit, waiting for whatever may befall them. The plague, a symbol of the unreasonable in nature that constitutes a permanent threat to the realm of the human, gains supremacy in proportion to the degree to which the inhabitants have abandoned the spirit, with its vigilant lucidity. A failure not unlike that of which Meursault is guilty.

From Rebellion to Conduct

With Meursault confronting death and opening up, "for the first time, to the tender indifference of the world," Camus has completed his dramatization of the development of the human spirit from complete immersion in the natural/social world to the emergence of the self-conscious and self-possessing individual. What remains is for such an emergent being to find a way to live. What meaning can a Meursault thus come unto himself find in his life? And what positive relations can he establish with his fellows? In this context we can appreciate the evocative explorations of the human condition encountered in *Nuptials*, and then the more argumentative theoretical exposition set forth in *The Myth of Sisyphus*. We would not be misled in viewing these works as the developing expressions of the being that Meursault has become.

I have already delineated the essential parameters of the Camusian vision. As natural animals we are extensions of the natural world with which we instinctively feel at one. But as conscious beings who can reflectively grasp the structure of that world, and of our distinctive place in it, we must recognize that our humanity is built upon the partial separation from nature of the realm of the human. We must, without imperiling our ties to nature, distance ourselves from its random course. And we must to some extent take upon ourselves the responsibility for the life we live. We must come to terms with our past and our future, incorporating into our lives the meaning that emerges from reflective appreciation of our finitude. We do not have unlimited time! Our potentially joyful union with nature will eventually be shattered by death. The "must" here is of course an ethical one. Meursault's rejection of the chaplain's consolations is not essentially negative. "There is a refusal which has nothing in common with renunciation. . . . If I obstinately refuse all the 'later-ons' of the world, it is as much a matter of not renouncing my present riches. . . . Everything that is proposed to me is an effort to discharge man of the weight of his own life. . . . Between the horror and the silence, the certitude of a death without hope . . . I understand that all my horror of dying comes from my jealousy for living" (*Noces*).

At this point, Camus explicitly refuses to view the absurd as a justification of resignation—as it had been for Sartre in "The Wall," of which Camus was quite aware at this time. In response to the chaplain's invitation to resignation, Meursault recapitulates Camus's response before the religious inscriptions in Florence: "'One must,' said the inscription. But no, and my revolt was right. This joy which was in process, indifferent and absorbed like a pilgrim on the earth, I had to follow it step by step. And, for the rest, I said no. I said no with all my strength. . . . I did not see what uselessness took away from my revolt and I know well that it added to it" (*Noces*). The revolt here articulated still lacks clarity as to what is being rejected—death, or the nihilistic resignation drawn therefrom—as well as a positive direction. Yet it has given forceful expression to the decision to affirm life in its present richness.

The conclusion of *The Stranger* is thus a beginning. Meursault now understands "why [his mother] had pretended to start over." We have come full circle. "Freed of the illusions of another life," our world has been returned to us fresh, inviting, uncertain, awaiting the significances we can give to it. The burdensome metaphysical and social rationalizations that fogged our vision and clogged our senses have been lifted. No wonder that sense of liberating release to which Meursault gives expression in opening up "for the first time, to the tender indifference of the world."

There can be little doubt that Camus personally felt the oppressive weight of social expectations and conventions, even to the extent of exhibiting traits of which he was not at all proud. The normal and expected, even the admired and rewarded, can often be quite violative of our self-respect and personal integrity. We can both play up to those expectations and at the same time be disgusted by so doing. The struggle to find acceptance, along with the distaste for such a need, can play havoc with a desire to be true to oneself. This tension plays like a basso continuo to the explicit themes of Camus's life and work. Thus Meursault's revolt is not only the metaphysical rejection of social hypocrisy, but also the personal purgation of the temptation to play by the rules—even to be the dandy—and the reaffirmation of the individual's right, experienced by Camus almost as a characterological duty, to be witness in one's actions to the truth of one's experience.

Meursault's revolt thus consummates a series of rejections:

- Of resignation in the face of death's inevitability.
- Of acceptance of the meaninglessness of a life without transcendence.
- Of any "leap of faith" in an afterlife *at the expense of* the only life we are given with certainty.
- Of the rituals of habit through which one's life is reduced to a meaningless routine—often rationalized in terms of a hoped-for life hereafter.
- Of the oppression of normal social order in which we are expected to be, feel, and behave in accordance with the "rules of the game."

The Stranger thus charts a pathway toward self-conscious affirmation, providing the metaphysical ground from which the positions first struggled with in *Two Sides of the Coin* and *Nuptials* and then reflectively articulated in *The Myth of Sisyphus* could emerge. It has cleared away the theoretical terrain, while existentially instantiating the necessary personal perspective. "*The Stranger* is the zero point," comments Camus. But it is to *The Myth* that I must now turn to begin to harvest the fruits of this perspective.

PETER SCHOFER

The Rhetoric of the Text: Causality, Metaphor, and Irony

Vous ne voulez pas? . . . Pourquoi? . . . J'ai dit 'Je ne sais pas'.
   Meursault explains why he did not want to view his mother's
   corpse.

*J'ai pensé qu'ils allaient aux cinémas du centre. C'était pourquoi ils
partaient si tôt et se dépêchaient vers le tram en riant très fort.*
   Meursault explains why people in the street were hurrying.

*Il m'a semblé que le ciel s'ouvrait sur toute son étendue pour laisser
pleuvoir du feu.*
   Meursault describes the instant before he killed the Algerian.

Why does he kill? How does he explain it? Those are two questions that
the reader is left with upon completing *L'Etranger*. Conventional wisdom
explains the book by appealing to the notion of the absurd: we cannot really
understand why he kills the Arab, and his manner of telling the story seems
only to confirm this explanation. The *Petit Robert* defines the 'absurd' as
'contraire à la raison, au sens commun'. There is little question that Meursault's crime was unreasonable and goes against common sense. He did not
know his victim, he was thrust in front of him almost by chance, and he is

From *Camus's* L'Etranger: *Fifty Years on.* © 1992 Macmillan Academic and Professional Ltd.

condemned for the wrong reasons. Yet is it all that absurd? Does not the text reveal something more than a vacuum around such important questions?

A close examination of the rhetoric of the story can dissipate much of the ambiguity surrounding the murder and can answer the two questions above. Words such as 'reason' and 'explain' imply the notion of causality—if we can see chains of cause and effect, we can then understand the event as being 'reasonable'. Although murder in itself is not a reasonable act, if we knew that Meursault hated the Algerian and that the Algerian had threatened him several times, the murder would seem 'reasonable'. It is that series of links which Meursault is incapable of supplying in his narrative and which leads us to seeing his act as 'absurd'.

Yet Meursault is quite capable of observing, understanding, and inferring causes. One of the best examples is the famous scene when Meursault spends a Sunday afternoon, immediately after the funeral, sitting on his balcony and observing activities in the street. Not only does he demonstrate that he has an acute sense of the smallest details, but he also deduces what the people are like, what they are doing, and where they are going.

Of a family man carrying a cane and wearing a bow-tie and boater, Meursault concludes 'j'ai compris pourquoi dans le quartier on disait de lui qu'il était distingué'. In the same passage, he sees people dressed up and running for the tram, concluding that they are going to the movies. The streets are then empty because 'les spectacles étaient partout commencés, je crois'. Later, he explains that the sudden outburst of people on the trams indicates that the soccer game is over. When the films are over, Meursault can even deduce that the spectators, by their forceful gestures, have seen an adventure film. He concludes his observations by noting 'c'était un dimanche de tiré'. Based on past experience and the habitual activities of a typical Sunday afternoon, Meursault can take pleasure in watching the streets and feel assured that he understands what other people are doing. Where there is an action, there is also a cause or motivation.

If he can draw conclusions seated on his balcony, at a distance from the participants, he does not show the same abilities when it comes to his own feelings and emotions. The passage in question ends rather astoundingly when he writes that 'c'était un dimanche de tiré, que maman était maintenant enterrée, que j'allais reprendre mon travail et que, somme toute, il n'y avait rien de changé'. *It occurred to me that anyway one more Sunday was over, that Maman was buried now, that I was going back to work, and that, really, nothing had changed.'* His mother's death is absorbed into the routine of weekly life, where his motivations and feelings become part of impersonal actions and activities. One might say that her death has not brought on any effects in his life.

This pattern is obvious throughout the book. Sometimes Meursault does put together cause and effect, but after the fact. On the first page of the book, when he asks his boss for time off, the latter does not seem happy with the request. It is not until the beginning of the following chapter that Meursault understands 'pourquoi le patron avait l'air mécontent quand je lui ai demandé mes deux jours de congé: c'est aujourd'hui samedi . . . Mon patron, tout naturellement, a pensé que j'aurais ainsi quatre jours de vacances et cela ne pouvait pas lui faire plaisir'; *'why my boss had seemed annoyed when I asked him for two days off: today is Saturday . . . And, naturally, my boss thought about the fact that I'd be getting four days' vacation that way, including Sunday, and he couldn't have been happy about that.'* But at other times he has no answer, as when he is asked directly why he does not want to see his mother's body.

At moments when one could expect him to examine motives, he is satisfied with accepting the sequence of events without questioning them. For example, after he learns that Salamano has lost his dog, he goes to his room and hears the old man crying. He writes: 'je ne sais pas pourquoi j'ai pensé à maman. Mais il fallait que je me lève tôt le lendemain'. *'For some reason I thought of Maman. But I had to get up early the next morning.'* Nowhere does he associate Salamano's loss with his own, nor does he see a causal link between Salamano's tears and his own repressed grief. He does write that he was not hungry and went to bed, but he does not ask himself why he is not hungry.

This same pattern of repression of causal links is clearly established from the moment he learns of his mother's death. One could expect that he would think of his mother while taking the bus to Marengo. Instead, he falls asleep and gives a clear reason: 'Cette hâte, cette course, c'est à cause de tout cela sans doute, ajouté aux cahots, à l'odeur d'essence, à la réverbération de la route et du ciel, que je me suis assoupi.' *'It was probably because of all the rushing around, and on top of that the bumpy ride, the smell of gasoline, and the glare of the sky and the road, that I dozed off.'* The accumulation of material causes almost acts as a sort of overkill to suppress any thinking and any introspection. As we will see later in an examination of the funeral procession, observation precludes any reflection about the effects of his mother's death on him directly.

This relative absence of causal links is intimately tied to the narrative style, where Meursault provides sequences of events but no causal links about his personal feelings. The following passage, during the wake, is typical:

Quand elle est partie, le concierge a parlé: 'Je vais vous laisser seul.' Je ne sais pas quel geste j'ai fait, mais il est resté debout derrière moi. Cette présence dans mon dos me gênait. La pièce était pleine d'une belle lumière de fin d'apres-midi. Deux frelons bourdonnaient contre la verrière. Et je sentais le sommeil me

> gagner. *When she'd gone, the caretaker said, 'I'll leave you alone.' I*
> *don't know what kind of gesture I made, but he stayed where he was,*
> *behind me. Having this presence breathing down my neck was starting*
> *to annoy me. The room was filled with beautiful late-afternoon*
> *sunlight. Two hornets were buzzing against the glass roof. I could feel*
> *myself getting sleepy.*

Although he says that the man's presence 'bothers' him, he does not explain why. As in the rest of the text, we are given a series of observations and actions without motivations. And, as in the bus, sleep overtakes him. Thus the scene of the murder is not at all exceptional except that it is a murder, not a narrative of banal events.

Causality does play an important role in the book however, particularly in the second half, which might be labelled 'displaced' or 'misplaced' causality. By its very nature, a trial not only seeks to establish facts, but it also establishes motives. Obviously, it is the function of the prosecutor, not the accused, to ascertain guilt and to assign motives; in other words to find reasons for the crime. As is well known, Meursault is condemned because he did not cry at his mother's funeral: he did not show the proper reaction to her death. According to society's conventions, death should be followed by its 'natural' effect, grieving. On a deeper level, Meursault's inability to grieve indicates that he has no heart, thus explaining his crime. Put another way, a lack of heart leads to the insensitivity toward his mother and towards the murder victim. One can read the second part of the book as a sort of double narrative, where Meursault continues to write directly of events and people, and where we try to figure out why he committed the murder. Specifically, at the trial most of the events from the first part of the book return, but now they are used to illustrate Meursault's heartlessness. Two examples suffice. In the first, the prosecutor summarizes Marie's testimony: 'Messieurs les jurés, le lendemain de la mort de sa mère, cet homme prenait des bains, commençait une liaison irrégulière, et allait rire devant un film comique. Je n'ai rien de plus à vous dire.' *'Gentlemen of the jury, the day after his mother's death, this man was out swimming, starting up a dubious liason, and going to the movies, a comedy, for laughs. I have nothing further to say.'*

Meursault would not have seen the events in that light, just as he only understands the following events through others:

> Il [le concierge] a dit que je n'avias pas voulu voir maman, que
> j'avais fumé, que j'avais dormi et que j'avais pris du café au lait.
> J'ai senti alors quelque chose qui soulevait toute la salle, et, pour
> la première fois, j'ai compris que j'étais coupable. *He [the*

concierge] said I hadn't wanted to see Maman, that I had smoked and
slept some, and that I had had some coffee. It was then I felt a stirring
go through the room and for the first time I realized that I was guilty.

It is worth noting that Meursault deduces his guilt from the reaction of the audience, not from the words of the concierge, nor from figuring out what he had actually done. As in the rest of the trial, actions which had been narrated as neutral, unmotivated events are transformed into indices of guilt. There is little question that a trial in which such evidence is admitted is an absurd trial, where reason is deflected into judging acts unrelated to the crime. Because of the way the second part of the novel folds back on the first part and imposes 'reasons' on Meursault's actions, and because of the way Meursault refuses to provide his own justification and motivations, the book apparently can be read in only one of two ways. Either we just accept the narration of sequential events or we throw up our arms and declare that it is all too absurd.

In novels, the 'best read' is perhaps the mystery story, where the reader is presented with a crime and is pushed along in his or her reading to discover who the criminal was, how the crime was committed, what instrument was used, and what the motivation was. A mystery writer teases the reader with false leads and misinformation as the reader seeks to tie up the chain of causal effects before the end of the book. In a good book, the answer does not come before the last page. *L'Etranger* is a mystery book gone askew. The criminal is known, the weapon is know, but motivation has to be contrived. The basics of a crime novel—discovering cause and effect—do not apply to this work.

If readings by causality produce no results, a metaphorical reading of the text can bear fruit. By metaphor, I mean metaphorical relationships, where semantic traits are shared by unlike words. They may be pure metaphors ('My flame') or comparisons, where terms are spelled out ('My love burns like a flame'). Metaphorical relationships can be found in the same sentence, in contiguous sentences, or on the same page. They can also be established between passages separated by many pages.

John Cruikshank has pointed out that the style in *L'Etranger* is very unrhetorical and that there are very few metaphors in the book. We can therefore assume that the presence of metaphors anywhere in the text is significant. The very first sentence, 'Aujourd'hui maman est morte', read in context alerts the reader to a metaphorical reading of the novel. Within the first paragraph, it is clear that the narrative does not capture the immediate present, because the second paragraph switches to the past tense, and the rest of the novel remains for the most part in the past. We are further warned that we should not take the first sentence literally when in the first paragraph the narrator says twice that the death was perhaps 'hier'. Logically we might deduce that the narrator does not know where he is, or we can look on his statement metaphorically: he is writing *as though* he were in the present, and he is reliving the experiences as though they were happening. In a sense, then, he is out of time and can put the events together. If we as readers ask 'Why did he do it?' and 'How does he explain it?', the narrator asks simply 'What happened?'. One thing happened: his mother died, and the memory, as he sits in prison, is as though it were today or yesterday.

The first metaphorical gesture is a subtle indication that under the broken causal strands there lurks a metaphorical reading of the entire novel. This reading has little to do with crimes, morals, or misdirected motives. It sees the novel in light of the first sentence, the death of a mother. As the narrator relives the past as though it were the present, he creates a double text. As we read the text before our eyes, we are asked to perceive the events in light of the mother's death *'today'*, as though today were yesterday and yesterday were today. The link between present and past, and between life and death, is metaphor.

Where do we go in the search of concrete metaphors in order to see how the double text is joined? According to Cruikshank,

> The very restrained character of Camus' vocabulary in *L'Etranger* leads to another interesting feature of his prose which was first pointed out by W. M. Frohock. There is one particular situation—Meursault's experience just before he shoots the Arab—which is described, not in severe and sober prose, but in a passage packed with metaphorical expressions.

Cruikshank explains this exceptional passage as an economical use of language to create a double purpose:

> He [Camus] uses the same set of words both to carry forward the narrative and to convey the psychological reasons for it. The accumulation of metaphors ultimately turns into a clever economy by which he dispenses with the necessity of treating narrative and motivation as two separate operations. He narrates in such a way that the motivation is implied without being explicitly formulated.

Cruikshank argues that the double structure of narration and metaphor can be explained as Meursault's hallucination:

> It is at this moment that Meursault suffers the final hallucination,

and his mental confusion becomes complete. The reader is encouraged to assume that he mistook the flash of light on the blade for the blade itself. Thus it seems as if Meursault really shot the Arab through an instinct for self-defense, an automatic reflex.

Cruikshank is quite right in seeing the double level of the passage, but by limiting his analysis to the passage itself, he fails to see the power of metaphor which permeates the entire text. At the moment that Meursault confuses the effect (the flash of light) and the cause (the Algerian holding the knife), causality is shattered and metaphor appears out of the rhetorical ruins. A comparison between the scene of the murder and the mother's funeral reveals strong metaphorical relationships. Let us first look at the vocabulary of the murder scene, presented here in a very schematic form and classified according to categories that the metaphors fall into:

> le soleil: écrasant . . . se brisaient en morceaux . . . a glissé . . .
>   sous la pluie aveuglante . . . le même éclatement rouge . . .
>   cette ivresse…
>   qu'il me déversait . . . se pressait . . . cymbales.
> la chaleur: s'appuyait.
> l'air: enflammé.
> le ciel: s'ouvrait sur toute son étendue pour laisser pleuvoir du
>   feu.
> le rocher: entouré d'un halo.
> le couteau: glaive éclatant.
> le mer: la poussière.
> la journée: avait jeté l'ancre dans un océan de métal bouillant.

While the metaphors are marked by extreme violence, they also represent a radical reversal of the natural order. The sea, which earlier represented a kind of rebirth when Meursault was swimming, is now dust. The sun and the air become driving, blinding rain; the knife itself is transformed into an exploding sword.

All the elements around him—the sun, the sky, the sea, and the rocks— are transformed into metaphors, but the Algerian, his presumed enemy, remains a literal entity, calm and 'content'. In no way, except for the presence of the knife, is he aggressive or actively threatening. If there is an absurdity in the passage itself, it resides in the situation before the killing: Meursault has a pistol and the Algerian has only a knife. It is the Algerian who is being menaced, whereas Meursault feels threatened, not by the Algerian, but by the intense heat and the inhuman sun. Meursault seeks refuge in the cool shadows and the murmur of the spring. He does not seek the Algerian, who is backing up. The Algerian is little more than a barrier to his need to find the shadows.

Since his mother's death, Meursault has encountered no barriers until he finds himself face-to-face with the Algerian. His has been in a flight from death and mourning. Upon his return to Algiers, he found Marie, went swimming with her, made love with her, resumed work, saw friends, etc. Now the order and sequences of everyday life are broken, and he finds himself confronting what he has sought to escape:

> C'était le même soleil que le jour où j'avais enterré maman et, comme alors, le front surtout me faisait mal et toutes les veines battaient ensemble sous la peau. A cause de cette brûlure, que je ne pouvais plus supporter, j'ai fait un mouvement en avant.

> *The sun was the same as it had been the day I'd buried Maman, and like then, my forehead especially was hurting me, all the veins in it throbbing under the skin. It was this burning, which I couldn't stand anymore, that made me move forward.*

Meursault clearly establishes a metaphorical relationship between the scene of the murder and the funeral when he says that it was the 'même soleil'. One might reply that it is obviously the same sun, since the earth has only one sun, but he explains that 'like then, my forehead especially was hurting me'. While he provides a link for the reader to the passage of the funeral, he also establishes causal parallels between the two scenes: the sun beats down and gives him an unbearable headache. In both cases, he moves forward.

Movement becomes a key. With all the differences between the funeral scene and the murder (the lack of the sea at Marengo, the prevalence of black, the flat surface), the most important is that of movement. At the funeral, he was in constant movement as he walked from the retirement home to the church. Now, he moves toward the blackness of the shadows. But the two movements are radically different: in the first scene, he walked toward the church, where his mother's death would be consecrated by the church, and where he would be faced with its finality. In the second, he walks toward the inverse of his mother's funeral, because he must kill in order to reach the security of the water (the source of life) and the shadows (the site of repose and the hint of death). In the first case, movement is like life—we move on. In the second, Meursault causes death when he can go no further.

If there are differences between the two passages, they remain tightly woven together, not just by the explicit quotation cited above, but by the similarity of key descriptive words. Let us look at the vocabulary to describe nature and Meursault's reaction to it:

le soleil: pesait, débordait, faisait trésaillir, inhumain, dépri
   mant.
le ciel: un éclat.
le front: des gouttes perlaient.
la terre: couleur de sang.
le chapeau: semblait avoir été pétri dans cette boue noire.
la campagne: gorgée de soleil.

As in the scene of the murder, the oppressive heat overwhelms him: 'me troublait le regard et les idées . . . Moi, je sentais le sang qui me battait aux tempes'. The expressions are highly metaphorical and suggest nature's violent effect on him: the sun 'weighed down', the sky was a 'flash', the earth takes on the color of blood, the countryside was 'filled'. Unlike his reaction at the murder scene, Meursault states that: 'je ne me souviens de rien'. Thus we are faced with similarities and differences. In the two scenes, the sun beats down so violently that he literally loses his head. At the funeral, there are signs of death everywhere, in the form of blackness—the black hats, the black of the road, and of course the black clothes. It would seem that objects became mud or sticky in the blazing heat. In both scenes, nature is alive and humans act as though they were dead. Meursault acts as though he were dead at the funeral, because on a real level he does not come to terms with death; it remains no more than signs. This realisation only comes to the surface at the instant that he shoots the Algerian, trans-forming his repressed grief into violence. In one case he forgets (represses), and in the other, he murders an innocent man. Both scenes represent a dead-end or an impasse, as is stated during the funeral, where 'il n'y avait pas d'issue'. The murder provides a double passage out of the sun and also out of the repressive bind, where his grief turns finally to violence.

For the reader, the metaphor of the sun can provide a way out of the impasse created by the movement of repressed grief to the violence of murder. Whereas the midday sun is represented in both passages as inhuman and maddening, on two other occasions, it stands for peace and tranquility. At the beginning of the funeral march, Meursault observes:

A travers les lignes de cyprès qui menaient aux collines près du ciel, cette terre rousse et verte, ces maisons rares et bien dessinées, je comprenais maman. Le soir, dans ce pays, devait être comme une trêve mélancolique.

Seeing the rows of cypress trees leading up to the hills next to the sky, and the houses standing out here and there against that red and green

> *earth, I was able to understand Maman better. Evenings in that part*
> *of the country must have been a kind of sad relief.*

The setting sun marks an end to the war of everyday life and provides a respite, a truce. Conventional symbolism associates the setting sun with the approach of death, here that of his mother, which Meursault interprets as a peaceful moment. Exactly the same words appear in the final paragraph of the book, where for the first time Meursault brings together his mother's death, his crime, and his own death. Appropriately, the passage occurs at night:

> Des odeurs de nuit, de terre et de sel rafraîchissaient mes tempes. La merveilleuse paix de cet été endormi entrait en moi comme une marée. . . . Pour la première fois, j'ai pensé à maman. Il m'a semblé que je comprenais pourquoi à la fin d'une vie elle avait pris un «fiancé», pourquoi elle avait joué à recommencer. Là-bas, là-bas aussi, autour de cette asile où des vies s'éteignaient, le soir était comme une trêve mélancolique. Si pres de la mort, maman devait s'y sentir libérée et prête à tout revivre. Personne, personne n'avait le droit de pleurer sur elle. Et moi aussi, je me suis senti prêt à tout revivre. Comme si cette grande colère m'avait purgé du mal, vidé d'espoir, devant cette nuit chargée de signes et d'étoiles, je m'ouvrais pour la première fois à la tendre indifférence du monde.

> *Smells of the night, earth, and salt air were cooling my temples. The*
> *wondrous peace of that sleeping summer flowed through me like a tide.*
> *Then, in the dark hour before dawn, sirens blasted. They were*
> *announcing departures for a world that now and forever meant nothing*
> *to me. For the first time in a long time I thought about Maman. I felt*
> *as if I understood why at the end of her life she had taken a 'fiancé',*
> *why she had played at beginning again. Even there, in that home where*
> *lives were fading out, evening was a kind of wistful respite. So close to*
> *death, Maman must have felt free then and ready to live it all again.*
> *Nobody, nobody had the right to cry over her. And I felt ready to live it*
> *all again too. As if that blind rage had washed me clean, rid me of hope;*
> *for the first time, in that night alive with signs and stars, I opened*
> *myself to the gentle indifference of the world.*

The above passage rewrites the previous ones referred to. The absent sun is replaced by the indirect sensations of smells of the night, the earth, and the sea. Metaphorically, the revitalising sea returns to him as a 'marvelous peace' (not a truce, as before), and enters him like a tide. He is now like his mother, united with her over time and death, and, like his mother, he is free to live again. For the two of them, the world is no longer violent, but rather 'indifferent'. However, Meursault achieves this indifference only because he had become angry with the priest and had purged himself. Significantly absent from this passage is any direct reference to the murder, because the crime now has significance only as part of the progression from negation to reconciliation with his birth and death. Murder stands as an intermediary between repression and acceptance of the void. The crime itself has been transformed into society's battle with Meursault.

If he is reconciled with his mother, he remains nonetheless alone and alienated by the injustices of his trial. To the end he has refrained from pronouncing the word 'amour', and the text ends on its opposite, 'haine.' A Lacanian might well point out that the two words are one. In any case, the unarticulated private love is transformed and deformed into its opposite and directed toward the crowd as it will observe his execution. Hate depends upon love, and love recalls hate.

While metaphor brings meaning out of the absurd, the text leaves open a number of ironies and unanswered questions. The most obvious, which Meursault broaches in his conclusion, is that he could not cry at his mother's funeral, because it would not, according to him, have been appropriate. No one had the right to cry. He could 'understand' his mother, yet he could never express his love directly, and his narration ends on hate. At the same time, the narrative itself is ironical, particularly for a person who relished the sea, sensuality, and the simple moments of life, all signs of a vital life. Ironical, because he learns to live in an enclosed cell, and he starts to live life only when he starts to write of it. Only through writing does he live. Writing brings deliverance where unarticulated love and hate of society have brought disaster. His new life through writing is also ironical because he had such difficulty talking with people. He tells us that he and his mother seldom talked. Now, only through writing can he speak of death and reconciliation.

The above reading of L'Etranger is ironical in the larger context of traditional readings of the text which emphasised the philosophical bent in Camus's thinking. To be sure, all texts contain a philosophical reading, but from the beginning to the end, L'Etranger is a highly personal confession in which the narrator arrives at self-knowledge while denying the validity of others in society, those Others beyond the Mother. Between birth and death is the Algerian, the Arab, the Other, the murder, and finally the hate of the Others. Toward the end of his life, Meursault notes that his execution will occur at sunrise: 'C'est à l'aube qu'ils venaient, je le savais.' He is secure in his knowledge that he will die when the sun is precariously balanced between black (hate) and light (love and understanding).

FRANTZ FAVRE

L'Etranger *and 'Metaphysical Anxiety'*

B y considering briefly the relationships of both Nietzsche and Camus to metaphysics, we will try to define what *L'Etranger* owes to Nietzsche. The existence of a debt at least cannot be denied, as Camus took care to warn us: 'C'est fini pour aujourd'hui, monsieur l'Antéchrist'. *'That's all for today, Monsieur Antichrist.'*

Such an assimilation of Nietzsche continues to surprise us. There is not, it would seem, any similarity between the moderation which Meursault habitually shows and the passionate violence of Nietzsche's attack on Christianity: 'I condemn Christianity! I bring against the Christian Church the most terrible accusation that has ever been uttered.' But what is more Nietzschean than Meursault's fidelity to the earth and his obstinate refusal of God. To the chaplain who asks him: 'Aimez-vous donc cette terre à ce point?' *'Do you really love this earth as much as all that?'* Meursault does not condescend to reply at all, as if he were imbued with Zarathustra's message: 'I implore you, my brothers, be true to the earth and don't believe those who talk to you about superearthly hopes.' Meursault seems to remember Zarathustra's following words—'they hold life in contempt, they are moribund'—when in his anger he shouts at the chaplain that 'il n'était même pas sûr d'être en vie, puisqu'il vivait comme un mort'. *'He wasn't even sure he was alive, because he was living like a dead man'.* There is, however, no trace of

From *Camus's* L'Etranger: *Fifty Years on.* © 1992 Macmillan Academic and Professional Ltd. (This essay was translated by Adele King.)

139

antitheism in this character whom we hardly see questioning himself about the strangeness of our condition. We can find in him a feeling neither of frustration nor of rebellion, nothing which usually nourishes the 'passionate disbelief' of the author. His final anger is directed against the chaplain, not against God. If it is true, as Schopenhauer says, that man is 'a metaphysical animal', the prosecutor is right to stress Meursault's inhumanity.

There is, on the other hand, a character in whom this 'metaphysical anxiety' is manifest: the examining magistrate. Undoubtedly he abuses the authority of his position to try to influence Meursault, but his nervous tics betray a real concern, and we cannot doubt the sincerity of his indignation and his incredulity when confronted by a disbelief that is so calmly stated:

> Il m'a dit que c'était impossible, que tous les hommes croyaient en Dieu, même ceux qui se détournaient de son visage. C'était là sa conviction et, s'il devait jamais en douter, sa vie n'aurait plus de sens.

> *He said it was impossible; all men believed in God, even those who turn their backs on him. That was his belief, and if he were ever to doubt it, his life would become meaningless.*

Such an admission, let us recognise, seems rather improbable. It proves, however, the existence of a mental attitude sufficiently prevalent to arouse Nietzsche's sarcasm:

> Egotism against Egotism: How many there are who still reach the conclusion: 'Life would be intolerable if God did not exist!' Or, as it is said in idealist circles, 'Life would be intolerable if it did not have an ethical foundation.' So, there must be a God (or an ethical foundation for life)! In reality it is completely different. A person who is used to this idea does not want to live without it; the idea is thus necessary for his preservation—but what a presumption to assert that everything necessary for my preservation must really exist! As if my preservation was necessary! What if others believed the opposite! If they refused to live accepting these two articles of faith, and if, these articles were true, life would no longer seem to them worth living! And that is how it is now!

Camus also placed himself in the lineage of Nietzsche when he wrote to Pierre Bonnell: 'I only object to believing that the need for a principle in metaphysics means that principle exists.' Without wanting to give undue credence to a too narrowly determinist notion of influences, which must be considered deeper the more they are diffuse, we could also be tempted to establish a link between the above citation from Nietzsche's *Dawn of Day* and the affirmation of *Le Mythe de Sisyphe:* Il s'agissait précédémment de savoir si la vie devait avoir un sens pour être vécue. Il apparaît ici au contraire qu'elle sera d'autant mieux vécue qu'elle n'aura pas de sens.' *'Before it was a question of knowing if life had to have a meaning in order to be lived. It seems here, on the contrary, that it will be lived so much better if it does not have any meaning.'* 'Lived better' (mieux vécue) because lived more freely and more intensely, with only the consciousness of death and the equivalence of all values. Here we rejoin Meursault and his certainty that he has lived as it is fitting to live.

What Meursault, in his anger, replies to the chaplain is less an argument than an affirmation of a certain way to live and to die. This should not surprise us as long as we remember the importance for both Nietzsche and Camus of the idea of a style of living. If, as Camus maintains, 'the only superiority as an example that Christianity has' lies in its 'search for a style of living', we can comprehend that the example of 'the only Christ we deserve' might belong, although in the opposite sense, to the same aesthetic order. The stylistic unity of Meursault's fate is based, like Nietzsche's proceeding, on an unfailing demand for truth. Certainly Meursault does not claim, like Nietzsche, to confront the dangerous problem of the meaning of this demand, and of the very value of truth. The goal towards which he climbs, however tragic its conclusion, takes more humble paths. The honesty which would be, according to Nietzsche, the 'ultimate virtue of free spirits' is not an honesty Meursault fulfills on the high summits of philosophical heroism, but rather at first in the routine framework of his daily existence. There he already shows a rare need for economy and accuracy of expression. 'C'est que je n'ai jamais grand chose à dire', as he will explain later to the examining magistrate. We might be astonished at the magistrate's reaction, as he says he is interested in Meursault but does not push this further and is satisfied with such an explanation. He hardly seems to suspect that there could be deeper reasons for Meursault's laconism and his refusal to use hyperbole. Everything takes place, however, as if Meursault, without formulating his position openly, distrusts the mythic function of language operating in what Robert Champigny has called 'theatrical society, antiphysis'. Convinced, like Nietzsche, that 'Every word is a prejudice', Meursault feels repelled by the need to use words. Faced by a court which, because it is caught in the trap of mythical language, fails to realise what is happening and indulges in the formal games of the judicial ritual so far as almost to forget the accused man, Meursault gives up trying to defend himself.

De temps en temps, j'avais envie d'interrompre tout le monde et de dire: 'Mais tout de même, qui est l'accusé? C'est important d'être l'accusé. Et j'ai quelque chose à dire!' Mais réflexion faite, je n'avias rien à dire.

There were times when I felt like breaking in on all of them and saying, 'Wait a minute! Who's the accused here? Being the accused counts for something. And I have something to say!' But on second thought, I didn't have anything to say.

Meursault's refusal to consider marriage as 'une chose grave' can be compared to this aphorism of Nietzsche:

'It is obvious, for instance, that a marriage is worth only as much as those who contract it, so in general a marriage has little value. As for "marriage itself", it has no value, nor does any other institution.'

The fictional world created by language cannot, however, be reduced to the single dimension of moral values and social conventions. Language orders our perception of the world, making it intelligible to us by projecting on the indistinguishable reality of what will happen a network of our logical categories. Nietzsche never stops insisting on the perfectly illusory character of our depiction of the world, which presumes the existence of acting substances and of causal links between identical phenomena:

We should not interpret the necessity we feel to create concepts, species, forms, purposes and laws (a world of identical cases) as if it would allow us to establish what the true world is; rather it is our necessity to adjust to ourselves a world which makes our existence possible; in this way we create a world that seems to us determinable, simplified, intelligible, etc.

Meursault's reluctance to explain himself, to oppose to the fictional but logical Meursault composed by the judiciary the real Meursault, would come then from his very Nietzschean conviction that 'nothing happening in reality corresponds strictly to logic'. This conviction is as well shared by the reader, whom the narrator, at the beginning of his story, has taken care to sensitize to the irrationality of the world through the atomized vision of a consciousness 'transparent to things and opaque to meanings'.

To this affirmation of the irrationality of the world is added a denunciation of the 'lie of faith in God'. This is a denunciation which, taking into account its philosophical implications or the gravity of the circumstances, can seem the highest accomplishment of that demand for truth which is common to Nietzsche and to Meursault, and the paradoxical source of which would be, according to Nietzsche, Christianity itself:

> We can see that what really triumphed over the Christian god was Christian morality itself, the idea of truthfulness that was applied with increasing strictness, the Christian conscience sharpened in the confessional and transformed into a scientific conscience, into intellectual cleanliness at all costs.

Although we can find Nietzschean elements in Meursault's rejection of the Christian god, if only in the pride of taking upon himself his own destiny—'Quant à moi, je ne voulais pas qu'on m'aidât', '*I didn't want anybody's help*'—Meursault's final violence seems to me to owe more to circumstances than to theory. He revolts less against Christianity than against the chaplain's will to impose his own belief. Without the awkward insistence of the priest, Meursault would probably have been satisfied with only his refusal to waste the little time he had left with God. But such indifference is undoubtedly more provocative than any hostility. Nothing is more significant in this respect than the incomprehension shown by certain Catholic critics, no matter how penetrating they can be in other matters, for whom this indifference can only be a 'numbness of conscience' which destroys 'what is most precious in man: his desire for transcendence'.

'That's all for today, Monsieur Antichrist' can therefore seem an attempt to create humorous distance, allowing the examining magistrate to arm himself against Meursault's disbelief, the provocative nature of which he had felt in such a passionate manner earlier. The naturalness of this attempt to make the situation less dramatic can, however, surprise us. The examining magistrate seems to have adapted himself to his Antichrist, who himself admits that he was taken in by the cordiality. Not that he was flattered by such a term, which hardly suits his nature, but because he has always shown himself to be sensitive to any display of sympathy and because he undoubtedly felt some satisfaction in seeing his disbelief treated with as much naturalness as he himself experienced it.

For it is indeed naturalness that characterises Meursault. By this we mean not only that simplicity and absence of prejudices shown by his conduct, but also—and more deeply—his reduction to *phusis*, to a state of consciousness, more mythic undoubtedly than real, which excludes neither sensitivity nor lucidity, but rather value judgements and 'metaphysical anxiety'. Nietzsche is perhaps again a source for such a character. Knowledge, he writes, does not necessarily lead to despair or to suicide. We can even imagine happy temperaments that accept it with detachment or serenity:

> A person would live finally among men and with himself as in nature, without praise, reproach, enthusiasm, taking delight as at a play in many things which formerly frightened him. He would be free from pomposity and would no longer feel the goad of thinking that he was not simply nature, or that he was more than nature. Of course, as I said, a good temperament would be necessary, a peaceful, mild and basically happy soul.

This airy lightness of spirit, which does not worry about the lack of meaning in existence, takes pleasure in 'soaring freely, without fear, over men, customs, laws and traditional evaluations of things'. This is a state Nietzsche strove to attain, that Nietzsche whose atheism is perhaps less precocious and less spontaneous than he likes to pretend:

> 'God', 'immortality of the soul', 'salvation', 'the after-life' are ideas to which I have not paid attention, with which I have not wasted my time [as Meursault refuses to waste his time with God], even when I was a child—perhaps I was not ingenuous enough for that! Atheism for me is not the result of something and still less an event in my life; it comes naturally, it is instinctive.

Undoubtedly Nietzsche forgot, in this late and somewhat rewritten self-portrait, the atmosphere of Protestant piety which had surrounded his childhood. He was more accurate—deeper—when he wrote:

> We are no longer Christian, we have gone beyond Christianity because we have lived not too far from it but too close and especially because it is from it that we issued; our piety, more harsh and more delicate at the same time, keeps us today from still being Christians.

It is nevertheless true that all the force of his philosophy tends to free us from the metaphysical-moral vision of being and from even the idea of God, 'the greatest objection to existence'.

It is tempting to oppose to this affirmation of radical atheism Camus's admission to Ponge: 'You got it right in your observation: it is true that I am

still a "nervous" man and that I cannot rid myself of metaphysical anxiety.'
Nietzsche seems indeed to have broken with metaphysics better than Camus.
Where Nietzsche's problem is to return man to himself and to reconcile him
with life, Camus poses questions on the way in which man, once returned to
himself in a world from then on absurd, can confront the injustice of his
condition and overcome his nostalgia for a metaphysical meaning: 'Savoir si
l'on peut vivre sans appel, c'est tout ce qui m'intéresse', *'Knowing if one can
live without calling out, that's all that interests me.'* (*Le Mythe de Sisyphe*) This
confrontation without hope is rebellion. The Camusian atmosphere can thus
be defined in its originality, its nostalgic frustrations and its rebellious
tension mixed, singularly, with lyrical impulses and a happy sensuality. We
are far from the grand Nietzschean 'yes' to *Amor fati*. In Nietzsche there is
no metaphysical rebellion in the sense Camus understands, but rather a
rebellion against metaphysics. Camus seems to interpret Nietzsche
according to his own problematic when he imagines at the origin of the
Nietzschean proceeding a metaphysical rebellion that Nietzsche would have
finally betrayed with *Amor fati*:

> Le oui nietzchéen, oublieux du non originel, renie la révolte
> elle-même, en même temps qu'il renie la morale qui refuse le
> monde tel qu'il est.

> *The Nietzschean affirmative, forgetful of the original negative,
> disavows rebellion at the same time that it disavows the ethic that
> refuses to accept the world as it is.*

What Nietzsche questions is less the human condition than man's attitude
towards his condition. It is not God who is guilty of injustice towards man,
but man who is guilty of injustice towards life. For Nietzsche it is a question
of freeing man from God, and not of raising a protest against him.

Meursault could have replied, like Camus, to the chaplain: 'The world
is beautiful and outside it, there is no salvation.' But in spite of the exclusive
love of this earth he shares with his author, he is surely more Nietzschean
than is Camus. When, at the threshold of death he feels 'prêt à tout revivre'
'ready to relive everything' and open with happiness to 'la tendre indifférence du monde', he consents, unlike Camus, to the great Nietzschean
affirmations of Eternal Return and *Amor fati*.

Such a surrender was not of course foreign to the author of *Noces*, who
admitted that 'au coeur de [sa] révolte dormait un consentement', *'at the heart
of [his] revolt consent is dormant'*. This consent could sometimes go as far as a
desire to become part of the mineral indifference of the world: 'Quelle tenta-

tion de s'identifier à ces pierres, de se confondre avec cet univers brulant qui défie l'histoire et ses agitations!' *How tempting to merge oneself with these stones, to mingle with this burning, impassive universe that challenges history and its agitations.'* Camus's temptation to join the world of stones is not of course without its Nietzschean precedent: 'How we should turn to stone—By becoming hard, very slowly, like a precious stone—and finally by staying there, peacefully, for the joy of eternity.' Camus's humanism, however, remains reticent when faced by these two fundamental concepts of Nietzsche's thought: Eternal Return and *Amor fati*. He can only accept the first by interpreting it in a sense that was surely not Nietzsche's, for whom Eternal Return is inclusive, not selective, and could not be reduced to commemorative echoes of 'des moments culminants de l'humanité', 'the highest moments of humanity'. And, for Camus, human nature itself seems incompatible with Nietzsche's second concept: 'C'est par le refus d'une partie de ce monde que ce monde est vivable? Contre l'Amor fati. L'homme est le seul animal qui refuse d'être ce qu'il est.' *'It is by refusing part of this world that we can live in this world? Against Amor fati. Man is the only animal who refuses to be what he is.'*

If it is true that 'the works of a man often retrace the history of his nostalgia or his temptations, almost never of his proper history', we can be permitted to see in *L'Etranger*, in spite of the subdued character of its hero, Camus's strongest Nietzschean 'temptation'. From the very fact that he pushes to the limit a refusal of any metaphysical concern, embodying it in the character of Meursault, Camus lets us see his own concern. The deepest paradox of *L'Etranger* would then be that Camus has entrusted to a 'natural' hero, one exempt form any painful conscience the duty of expressing, through its opposite, his 'metaphysical anxiety'.

STEPHEN ERIC BRONNER

Meursault

The three absurds," Camus could note in his journal entry of February 21, 1941, "are now complete." He was speaking about *The Stranger*, *The Myth of Sisyphus*, and *Caligula*. The first is a novel, the second an essay, and the third a play. Together they represent the literary range of Camus. The three were written around the same time, and, in his mind, they became linked by a word: the absurd. Of these three works, *The Stranger* is the best known. Finished in 1940, it did not appear until 1942. Finding a publisher was not easy. Camus was still virtually unknown in France, and, supposedly, André Malraux "imposed" the novel on the major French publisher Gallimard. It is now viewed as a classic. Few such genuinely enigmatic works, which distance even while they emotionally engage the reader, have ever had this kind of success. Perhaps it seduces with its strange egoism. It was surely considered new in its style. Although it is rarely considered this way, however, it actually presents a modern form of the "educational novel" (bildungsroman).

The Stranger fuses the modernism of André Malraux and the classical prose of André Gide with an exoticism both often shared in their writings. The detachment of its author and main character also owes much to American authors like Ernest Hemingway and James Cain. But it doesn't intentionally celebrate cynicism, nihilism, or the loss of values—quite the contrary. Its close is a celebration of the lived life, and the novel deals with the trans-

From *Camus: Portrait of a Moralist.* © 1999 Regents of the University of Minnesota.

formation of an indifferent yet self-absorbed individual, a man committed to remaking his life in the shadow of death.

Meursault, the main character, initially appears disinterested in anything other than immediate physical sensations and honesty. He doesn't care about money or promotions and displays no emotions when his mother dies. He expresses no feelings at her funeral, other than discomfort in the heat, but he notices the most incidental objects like the screws in the coffin and the clothes people are wearing. The day of the funeral is a day like any other, and on the morrow he goes swimming, where he meets a young girl whom he seduces and then takes as his mistress. Maria Cardona, who bears the name of Camus's grandmother, asks him to marry her and he agrees. Meursault is polite but remains emotionally distant.

One choice is as meaningless as the next and encounter follows encounter. Meursault goes again to the beach with his fiancée and his friend Raymond Sintes, whose last name echoes that of Camus's mother, along with Sintes's girlfriend. He says nothing when his friend beats his girlfriend. They chance upon a group of Arabs, who have a score to settle with Sintes, a pimp and a tough. Words are exchanged, the men scuffle, then everyone disperses. Blinded by the sun and looking for a spot of shade, however, Meursault returns and meets one of the Arabs, who flashes a knife. Meursault fires a shot, then four more. The Arab lies dead. The police arrest Meursault. He is put on trial and condemned to death. But the reason for this extreme judgment has little to do with the murder. In Algeria, with the racist attitudes of the French colonial administration, such an act would normally receive only a few years of imprisonment. The real reason the jury condemns Meursault stems from his refusal, under cross examination, to explain his actions or to lie about his inability to weep at his mother's funeral. This "stranger" from himself and society now waits for death. In prison, Meursault makes use of his memories and forgets the boredom that had defined his previous existence. The chaplain comes and is turned away.

Camus had already written in his notebooks, in 1935 and 1936, that he was considering composing a story about a "man who refuses to justify himself." *A Happy Death* is that story, but his new character, Meursault, is that man. Society must elicit a reason for his actions, and since he refuses to provide one, the prosecutor portrays him as a cold-blooded psychopath. In fact, his act of murder is neither more nor less arbitrary than any of his other more human experiences. Camus takes great pains to show that there is no objective answer for *why* Meursault killed the Arab. It was a "gratuitous act," an act without reason or justification, which incidentally has its own literary tradition in Dostoyevsky, Gide, Malraux, the surrealists, and others. The act without purpose indeed mirrors a world without meaning.